W9-AZK-901

What Can Be Done Now to Save Habitable Life on Planet Earth?

Leaders Commit to Reduce Human Population

Donald A. Collins Publishing

Washington, D.C. 20015
Phone: (202) 656-6421

Edited by Donald Collins, Jr.

Published by Donald A. Collins Publishing 10/31/2021

ISBN: 9798756176292

Print information available on the last page.

This book is printed on acid-free paper.

Dedication

Dedicated to Sarah G. Epstein with whom I've shared a
blissful journey for 27 years.

Carolyn Newman

with Love

Don Colflesh

Contents

Introduction

Vision-less world leadership has led our Earth to a point of no return to the possibility of safe human habitability. The UN Climate meeting in Scotland next week will either show a wake-up call, but more likely just talking and just another step toward the future which our lack of action has been long predicted.

Sir David Attenborough, the distinguished film maker and environmentalist, will speak at this Climate meeting, but his earlier cautions on climate and population issues have been ignored by world leadership. His documentary and his advice that the climate issue must be urgently dealt with now or it will be unsolvable, will not likely be addressed enough.

Thus, the current bad news I mention first here will soon seem so much less important as will the overpopulation issue I cover below.

For example, I am more convinced that Putin's influence on Trump's election in 2016 was greater than any other secret attacker including Facebook's, based on Trump's subsequent cuddling up to Putin, saying he trusted him more than some of his own advisers.

The exact reasons for Trump's sellout to Putin are not known now, but that history will be revealed at some point.

Will Trump's political future collapse before 2024. Few predict that happening, but surely his lying, self-interested behavior may turn off some of his supporters.

But as far as the weaknesses in our democracy are concerned, we can't blame Trump totally for what allowed him to be elected.

And more and more voters on both sides of the aisle are getting sick of his manic repetition of voting fraud and his willingness to commit any crime to lead to his re-election. Read here the growing disaffection about his lying as possibly hurting the election of Trump's House or Senate doxies.

Further, as the House commission of January 6th continues, more evidence piles up. For examples, the Rolling Stone article reports active coordination of the insurrection from a suite at the nearby Willard Hotel with White House staffers and other related stories, which you can read here:

1. "EXCLUSIVE: Jan. 6 Protest Organizers Say They Participated in 'Dozens' of Planning Meetings With Members of Congress and White House Staff," Rolling Stone, October 24, 2021

2. "House votes to hold Trump ally Steve Bannon in criminal contempt for defying subpoena," CNN, October 21, 2021

3. "Jan. 6 committee chair: 'No question' Capitol riot was a premeditated attack," The Hill, October 25, 2021

4. "The 14th Amendment's Disqualification Provision and the Events of Jan. 6," Lawfare, January 19, 2021

Fiona Hill, in her landmark book, "There Is Nothing For You Here—Finding Opportunity In The 21st Century" has explained so succinctly how the pockets of poverty allowed Putin to promise his citizens better lives in Russia before he established his dictatorship and Trump, trying the same tactics starting with his lies with his Make America Great Again speeches and now with his continuing claims of voter fraud despite his extensive efforts to overturn Biden's substantial election margin.

In short, the gun for disaster was already loaded and all Trump did was pull the trigger. And as in the recent sad case on the Rust movie set, their gun's bullet was supposed to be a blank, but these guns are real and deadly, as climate change and human overpopulation issues are already seriously endangering the world.

Let's understand another issue which will dominate the disgraced GOP's continuing Biden attacks: Immigration. Instead of understanding what daily media reports show us—that the immigration gun is already loaded—we and all the wealthier nations of the world keep ignoring that the real solutions must focus on keeping migrants from desperately needing to migrate. Do we need a new

Marshall Plan as after WWII?

Now, instead of backing or ignoring the vicious dictatorships that corruptly use our foreign aid to augment their wealth and power, the U.S. should be trying to organize a consortium of nations who would first identify the corrupt nations in their orbits for real improvement. In our case, the Central American nations, Costa Rica would be a model for the other poorly functioning nations there.

We could require for any foreign aid the right to monitor and audit these dictatorships. If they refuse, we could not allow their citizens to get visas to come to the USA or gain asylum after they enter the U.S. illegally.

Wild idea? Difficult? Of course, but we are already deep into the dangerous world of overpopulation, as humans, particularly from rich nations, continue ravaging Earth.

Overpopulation remains Earth's fundamental problem. Understand that fixing our climate may not be possible, even starting urgently now, and more technology won't solve this too many people problem as we add a net 80 million humans to Earth yearly.

The absurdity of allowing Trump to further damage our fragile democracy becomes clearer daily, but the urgent need to reduce human impact on Earth is even more clear to our scientists but ignored by those in power around the world.

Imagine two Democrat senators now hold our democracy in the palms of their self-interested hands. Sadly, the vision-less GOP leadership is worse. Biden's bills, if enacted, may be too little, too late, and have little bearing on our real problems.

I'm not optimistic about our future.

So why another book about facts which are now so well proven? Simply to raise the level of understanding of my Op Ed readers and other possible audiences and state an urgency for repair before time passes and all is lost.

Also, to acknowledge that the text, sans the substantial electronic options which were added, allows me to offer my heartfelt thanks for years of support to my editors Declan and Lola Heavey, whose powerful web site located in London has support from 63 Nobel Prize laureates who come from 20 Honorary Associates, eight articles, nine book excerpts, and 33 stem cell petition signatories. Church and State has 308 Honorary Associates and other credible experts on a variety of cogent topics. Go to www.churchandstate.org.uk for my material and to see other visionary materials.

Donald A. Collins
Washington, DC.
October 31, 2021

Chapter 1 How Trump's 30 Percent Of Core Supporters Could Expand By 2024!

23 October 2021

How can the fealty for Trump and the felonious behavior of the GOP leadership be sustained with all we know about his despicable character and the failure of moral Leadership by the GOP?

From the recent testimony before Congress by the former Facebook employee who had taken irrefutable evidence from Facebook's own files, Congress showed bi-partisan fury at how Facebook allowed false hate invoking material to be broadcast. We all now know that's where Facebook's most profits were made.

Regulation may follow, but that's not what got Trump his votes in the first place or what is keeping their loyalty now.

Fiona Hill's new book, "There Is Nothing For You Here— Finding Opportunity In The 21st Century" covers her attacks from Trump, but is not primarily about Trump, rather about what she believes led to the destruction of millions of jobs and communities when technology changed creating pockets of poverty like the community she grew up in in England where her father told her, "There is nothing for you here".

Seeing the terrible effect in Russia, where she learned Russian, and became an expert policy analyst then further gained an extensive education including a Harvard Ph.D., resigned as a policy advisor to the Trump White House.

Primary point: she compares the Russian experience that gave Putin his path to dictatorial power to what she sees possible in the US, as many more Americans feel themselves in these pockets of poverty that she grew up in.

As we know such pockets of poverty also lead to poorer health and resentment which was in her view a key basis for Trump support in 2016. Only his aberrant behavior saved us from his second term in which bad voting rights legislation could have been cemented and that would be again if he gets another chance.

The poor often don't have internet connections, so they are perfect targets for false information from the Trumps of this world. Even with the education part of Biden's final package deleted, passing the two pending bills is crucial to keep the Democrats in power after the midterms.

Chapter 2 <u>President Biden Talks To Us In Person And Straight In His Town Meeting</u>

22 October 2021

On CNN's one and half hour program on Thursday evening October 21 alone on a stage with host Anderson Cooper, I watched a powerful presentation by a man fully connected and conversant with the dazzling and confusing array of current issues, but also very hip on the future implications of doing nothing to improve our nation's future, as is the case with the current GOP.

Perhaps for first time in a long time I felt much more as though I was having a personal conversation with the President. His words, based on the applause of his admittedly invitation only audience, but also in the expectant faces of those who were asking him very pointed questions, seemed to me to be ringing true to his audience.

Biden, in taking those hard questions from this audience and Cooper, replied in a clear and plausible way, often prefacing his answers by saying, "Here's the deal."

It was to me a bravura performance showing, as I repeat for emphasis, a President in full knowledge of the

3

complex situations he is dealing with, and hopefully will be able to move forward on, despite the split within his own party and the flagrant opposition of the non-governing GOP.

Americans, in the opinion of many experts, are at a crossroads which is so clearly and ominously described in Fiona Hill's new book, "There Is Nothing For You Here—Finding Opportunity In The 21st Century". She describes the wide spreading absence of educational opportunity, as the traditional heavy industries in many countries vanished. Those left behind in pockets of unemployment or low paying jobs became willing to embrace the lying mouthings of Trump and causing the most disaffected among them ultimately to storm our Capitol on January 6th only to continue to be told and believe his lies thereafter.

You can read Fiona Hill's story and her ominous contention that populism as offered by Trump—absent educational and reasonable employment opportunity for all will allow the continuing increase in that present 30 percent of our citizens who will continue to buy the lies and fantasies that Trump types offer.

This positive course is what Biden is hoping to achieve.

Read the fascinating Washington Post review on Fiona Hill entitled "The rare Trump insider memoir that doesn't obsess over Trump" here.

She depicts a really dangerous and little understood trend in the USA.

Biden also noted this educational need to help improve conditions not only here but in places; for example, such as Central America to help reduce their citizens' impetus to migrate.

Could this help to other nations, carefully monitored for effectiveness, be the only true path for a global solution to population reduction allowing all humans choices for a more viable future. Not forced to accept religious or authoritarian orthodoxy or fantasies of those seeking personal power that demand ignoring healthy choices based on scientific knowledge.

As Biden told his Town Hall audience "Just K though 12 education is not enough".

Chapter 3 <u>Trump Tried To Do A Coup On January 6th While President. How Is He Not in Jail?</u>

21 October 2021

To me some of the most telling quotes about Trump's January 6th behavior came from Colin Powell in an interview with Bob Woodward. You can read a brief piece <u>here</u>.

Trump's disgraceful moral character while amply documented before January 6th was sufficient to earn him two impeachments, which should have resulted in his conviction, the first President in U.S. history to be thrown out of office as Powell suggested he should have been. It would have happened, but for the GOP sycophants who now have helped Trump destroy the credibility of the GOP, and now go forward trying to enfeeble or dominate our democracy.

An article by Jackie Calmes in the LA Times succinctly and sharply repeats the obvious division between the morality of Colin Powell and his Republican successors. Read it <u>here</u>.

The irony of Trump's felonious attempts to hide behind our precious rule of law, as has been dramatically exhibited with his multiple attempts to elude the House of Representatives January 6th Commission's probe into the facts of what happened.

The indictment of Steve Bannon is a positive step, but the road to proving Trump's guilt is not yet clear.

My main point remains that the heart of keeping our democracy viable rests with the integrity of its elected officials. Absent that quality as the predominant influence in the conduct of our affairs, we will be soon lost as a functioning democracy, but like countless other countries, bragging about being democratic while being headed by de facto corrupt dictatorships.

Not indicting and convicting this former Felon-in-Chief could insure such a path for our democracy.

Chapter 4 What Can Be Done Now To Save Habitable Life On Planet Earth?

20 October 2021

Reading or listening to events of the day can be very depressing, particularly if you are not deeply preoccupied with daily jobs or compelling avocations.

Even at 90, as I am, asking the above profound question, as I do constantly, does keep energizing me.

My earlier Op Ed pieces on planetary ills can be revisited on this site, which is so richly endowed by its principal editors with the writings of others on topics which profoundly influence the chances for the habitability of our human species on an earth we have so fecklessly savaged.

Seeming unawareness of the urgency of these looming threats by so many Americans, makes me pessimistic about a happy ending!

The list provided by a bright and informed family member of mine and contained in my recent Op Ed is repeated here to allow my augmenting comments below her list.

"Our nation's situation and the slow chipping away & destruction of our democracy have become so disheartening, so negative, so frightening that many former politically savvy individuals are so turned off right now, so dismayed & discouraged that choosing not to watch the news in order to maintain one's sanity has become the day-by-day reality.

It all seems so overwhelmingly apocalyptic.

Yes, we can protest, write, support political candidates whose views reflect ours–but once elected look at what they and we face in terms of governing.

Climate Change

Trumpism

Racism

The Pandemic and those to come

Wildfires, Hurricanes, Floods

Sexism

Inequitable distribution of wealth

Poverty

480 million refugees worldwide....and on and on...."

What my well informed relative well knows and could have added to her list of concerns was their universality. Think of the conditions on her list and realize they depict the worldly human failings. Including Trumpian type leaders and worse.

The absence of so many of the citizens of the world to recognize or urgently act on these onrushing calamities should be frightening, but seems to most people to be just something that can be dealt with, like climate. The rest of the world needs help as you can read here.

As for poverty, here is daunting data to read.

The world seems almost lackadaisical as we pursue our lifestyles without doing what we are being told by science or acting on its findings with proper funding.

Current leaders like Senator Manchin, who says the budget is too high, and doesn't want to limit the coal companies who provide over 90% of the electricity to his home state of West Virginia. And no one is quite sure what Arizona Senator Sinema wants except less essential funding. Will we lose Congress in the midterms? The failure of Biden's program and even getting a disastrous Trump replay in 2024 will seem in retrospect to be minor failures if attention is not paid to population limitation.

As for immigration, those poverty-stricken millions will keep coming to richer countries unless the world's rich can keep those poor people in their homes with some semblance of habitability. If we and other capable powers don't act, in the near future, this all will seem minor.

The current situation makes me wonder what my grandchildren and their offspring will face if, as the eminent naturalist Sir David Attenborough predicts, by 2100, that, Folks, is just in 79 years (one average human lifetime) from now, there will be 11 billion humans, instead of the nearly 8 billion here now, all competing for the less abundant resources than we have now. You can read my recent book on the population problem.

We humans as a species MAY have already passed planetary fixability and possible survival. Are humans, largely unknowingly, plummeting into a territory of living conditions previously unknown to us? Well, as you know, the large dinosaurs who dominated the earth went extinct around the time a meteor hit the Yucatan 66 million years ago. While a lot of lesser species survived, it only took those millions of years to get our species up and running. So why worry, right?

11

Chapter 5 China's Premier Chi Implies With COVID His System Works Better Than Our Democracy

18 October 2021

If asked before our democratic system elected Donald Trump, a majority of Americans would undoubtedly have said we do better than China.

We can hope that would prevail today, although Chi obviously believes his dictatorship works better. For example, read how China handles COVID here.

In this article, its repressive approach, of which it is proud, but "Mr. Xi (bathed in glory, he surely hopes, for his victory over covid) will use as a launching pad for five more years, at least, in office", even though its vaccines are inferior to ours.

My very much "woke" relative recently emailed me her despairing analysis, which you can read here, which strongly echoes my own:

> "Our nation's situation and the slow chipping away & destruction of our democracy have become so disheartening, so negative, so frightening that many former politically savvy

individuals are so turned off right now, so dismayed & discouraged that choosing not to watch the news in order to maintain one's sanity has become the day-by-day reality.

It all seems so overwhelmingly apocalyptic.

Yes, we can protest, write, support political candidates whose views reflect ours–but once elected look at what they and we face in terms of governing.

Climate Change

Trumpism

Racism

The Pandemic and those to come

Wildfires, Hurricanes, Floods

Sexism

Inequitable distribution of wealth

Poverty

480 million refugees worldwide....and on and on...."

Our now one-party governing Democrats can't even get its own members to pass desperately needed legislation because the vision horizons of a few of its members don't go beyond their personal political fortunes. Their intransigence will cost lives and possibly lead to loss of Congress in the midterms.

Is the only way to manage a feckless or too numerous population the way Chi does it?

China's population numbers have tripled since WWII to 1.4 billion.

Our numbers have gone from 130 million to 340 million since my birth in 1931.

Perhaps most disturbing is the fact that a sitting President tried to stage a coup to stop his elected successor from taking office and has not yet gone to jail for his felonious crime. This may be the best current example of how our democracy has failed.

Another outrageous example of democracy's failure is Trump's and McConnell's (remember the latter's blocking of the Obama appointment of Merrick Garland to the U.S. Supreme Court?) destruction of the Supreme Court, as the 5 to 4 majority likely moves toward killing Roe.

As Wikipedia tells us, "Abortion in China is legal and is a government service available on request for women. Although this does not, in theory, apply to sex-selective abortion, it remains the basis for some women's requests. In addition to virtually universal access to contraception, abortion was a common way for China to contain its population in accordance with its now-defunct one-child policy, which was removed in 2015 in favor of a two-child policy, which in turn was replaced in 2021 by a three-child policy."

Read more about China's abortion policy here.

Then, see our failure to fix immigration! New immigrants for our nation have always been badly needed. Just look at the mixed foreign ethnicity of our Nobelists and other innovators, but the fixing has failed due to politically motivated business (cheap labor), religions (more of one faith over another) and the obvious draw of foreigners here because of our success SO FAR as a nation (remember we are the "land of opportunity"), we keep a laissez-faire open border policy which makes excess numbers certain to exceed our needs.

In summary our next era as a democratic nation is in serious doubt and only with substantial courage and generosity of spirit will we overcome the venal Trump's continuing cancerous influence.

Chapter 6 Citizens Awaken! You Have Nothing to Lose but Your Life

17 October 2021

This last Thursday morning, a bright sunny Fall Day in DC, my doorbell rang and when I answered, a well-dressed young, uniformed man, masked, had come from his company, as someone from his company has for many years, to do routine maintenance on our heating/air conditioning system.

I asked if he had been vaccinated and he replied he had not, at which point I politely said he could not come in. Equally courteously he replied, "No problem, Sir. I'll have them send someone who is vaccinated" and drove away. I appreciated his telling me the truth and wondered how long he would get to keep his job.

Over 60 million Americans have not yet been vaccinated and of those who get COVID over 97 percent of the deaths are to those people who are unvaccinated.

Those of the few vaccinated ones, including one of my friends, 83, who after having been vaccinated twice, still contracted COVID, was put on a ventilator and after 8 days died in September. My wife and I continue to wear masks anywhere we go in public and will be getting our third booster shot shortly.

I report this rare incident to stress the failure of too many of us, not just the weak bulbs who aren't yet vaccinated, but to the mindless failure to understand the precarious situation we and everyone here and in the world is in.

The best article I have seen on this topic was Philip Bump's October 10, 2021 piece, entitled "How many thousands of people are choosing death over vaccination?"

Here's just the first paragraph:

> "There is a chain of events that has almost certainly happened at least once in the United States this year. A person eligible for a coronavirus vaccination decides against getting it, having seen articles in right-wing media or coverage on Fox News misleadingly or falsely downplaying the efficacy and safety of immunization. That person has then contracted covid-19 and died."

It's really hard to blame the Biden Administration for the burgeoning of Delta, but frightening that his chief advisor, NIH's Dr. Anthony Fauci, whose outstanding advice all through this pandemic, now requires full time security protection after numerous death threats from Trump supporters.

The origin of the pandemic was after all the product of the Trump Administration, which despite the heroic accomplishments of Pfizer and other drug firms, still failed to stress masking and distancing and kept holding unmasked meetings until Trump got COVID and was given special treatment which led to his recovery so he could continue to appear unmasked in public, even as he extolled his core supporters to stage an insurrection on January 6th.

Will enough of us fail to grasp Senator Grassley's and the majority of the Trump GOP's gross greed or stupidity to misunderstand the continuing Trump agenda with his GOP's push to authoritarian power, beginning with the midterms in 2022 or his possible third run for the Presidency in 2024?

Somehow, one gets the scary feeling that none of his fascist style faults have registered as a distinct possible reality with enough of us in both parties.

Chapter 7 <u>Humans' Habitable Survival On Earth Lessens As We Ignore All Advice...</u>

15 October 2021

The evidence is clear and has been for some time that human life on Earth is under huge pressure, getting worse daily.

One critical piece of danger is the behavior of our polar ice caps as NOVA has told us about the findings in the Arctic in a recent U.S. and Russian led study.

The spate of unusual weather events everywhere, which this report and others can be proven to be related, the shrinking of the ice cap in Arctica has already drastically changed weather patterns worldwide. Read the NOVA story, entitled 'Arctic Drift' Review: In Search Of Cold, Hard Facts, partly covered <u>here.</u>

Meanwhile, the U.S. Congress, absent any constructive input from one of our two governing political parties, dithers about taking significant action on climate, so as the elected members of the GOP believe, we don't spend too much money on our survival!

What if we did undertake a major climate effort? Such major leadership might encourage the other major polluters around the world to join us which would up the odds of our dubious prospects for saving habitable life, even as the number of uneducated, poor, and desperate people on Earth keeps increasing.

As for the aspirant nongoverning party, the GOP, led by visionless Mitch and ring kisser Kevin who want the power of re-election more than retaining a working democracy, they're clearly incapable of understanding (as too many others are) the future of a world whose humans increased by 6 billion in my 90-year lifetime

And nothing the media reports, or the countless warnings from reputable scientists, or what the evidence of history amassed by many respected scholars of social commentary tells us, seems to rouse the sleeping masses. Sadly, most of the world's leaders know the facts of what has happened and will very soon happen to make life on Earth increasingly uninhabitable.

Whatever one thinks of Mr. Biden, the comparison to his immediate predecessor, who would bring us a new version of authoritarianism, seems to have eluded the understanding or the willingness to act of too many of our citizens.

Chapter 8 <u>Judging Heroes Can Be Tricky, But Not In Trump's Case</u>

13 October 2021

I regularly read the Wall Street Journal opinion pages just so I know what the arguments are coming from the political right. Notice I didn't say "hard or deep right", although I sometimes wonder. When a fair WSJ piece appears, I am delighted and appreciative.

Such was the case of Garry Kasparov's October 11th opinion piece entitled "Celebrate Columbus's Achievements" which begins "Friends, American citizens of the world, l come to bury Columbus not to praise him". He then cites his analogy to Marc Antony's eulogy of Caesar which allows Antony's subtle attack on Caesar's attackers who were fearful of his burgeoning power, much as most thinking Americans now feel about Trump.

Speaking of heroes to admire, one is certainly <u>Garry Kasparov</u>, a Russian, probably the world's greatest chess player ever, who since retiring from competitive chess, has proved most brave in his assaults on Putin's dictatorship. Considering Putin's treatment of other Russian dissidents, such as Alexei Navalny, Kasparov's present NYC residence is no surprise.

His main point is that we should mark the flaws of historical heroes (presume heroines as well), but not overlook their accomplishments. Read his Op ED here.

I agree with that, but in the case of Civil War statuary allowing Lee and Jackson to posthumously keep flaunting their racist history in the faces of African Americans after 400 years of racism is no longer to be tolerated.

Kasparov's analogy had earlier prompted my poetic doggerel attempt to express my urgent hope for Trump's political eulogy!

Here, thanks to Marc Antony, is my modest effort about the most dangerous President in U.S. history: DAC on Trump ala Marc Antony's eulogy of Caesar.

Friends, Enemies, U.S. Citizens, lend me your ears
I have come to vilify Trump, not to praise him
The evil this man has already done in his life
Will be well remembered long before he is dead
So don't let his sins be buried by his lying
That Trump is ambitious needs no retelling
It is a grievous fault, but not his worst fault
And so far, he has not answered for them
Except by failing to win reelection in 2020
Here I leave others to judge his life and the
Books written by experts make an iron case.

But for sure Trump is not an honorable man
Nor are most of his closest tribe honest men
But all of them are completely ambitious
And all claim falsely to be honorable men
Hath Trump brought to us many other costs
Including Government use of his DC hotel
Was this ambition or just conflict of interest?
As his cult members cheered his ego was assuaged
But many saw he was never an honorable man
When elected in 2016, did he just start being evil
No, just getting to use his crown for personal power
Which he never failed to use for his personal gain
Were these actions examples of his ambition?
Not that he ever was an honorable man
I speak not to laud this lying traitor
But only speak of what is in the public record
But even now his supporters still love him
Particularly elected traitors to fawn at Mar-A-Lago
Who seek re-election without caring for democracy?
Which is now their only reason to love him
Will you mourn him when he is finally found out?
Will you apologize for your loss of faith and duty?
My heart hopes that by then we are still a democracy

Can my country survive Trump until then?

But watching the squirming GOP leadership still
denying the impact of January 6th, as perhaps, some

commentators have suggested, a great dress rehearsal for more violence in the future which could make Trump's attempted coup happen, if he runs again and loses again.

Or worse, Trump runs in 2024 and gets elected! A true scary echo back to Hitler's route to authoritarianism. The loss of our democracy is now on the line, as the few responsible GOP leaders fail, fail, fail. Are they all honorable men? The 2022 midterms could decide.

Bill Maher offers an even more pointed prediction which you can read in full here.

> "TV host Bill Maher on Friday predicted the role that former President Donald Trump could have ahead of the 2024 presidential election, and suggested that Capitol Hill rioters would return stronger than they were on January 6.
>
> On his show Real Time with Bill Maher, Maher offered his "dark prediction" of a "slow-moving coup" that he believes Trump is currently preparing for an attempt to take back the White House. This includes Trump trying to gain the Republican nomination and announcing his presidential candidacy.
>
> "I've been saying ever since he lost. He's like a shark, that's not gone, just gone out to sea. But

actually, he's been quietly eating people this whole time. By eating people, I mean he's been methodically purging the Republican Party of anyone who voted for his impeachment, or doesn't agree that he's the rightful leader of the Seven Kingdoms," Maher said.

He also suggested that Trump supporters who raided the Capitol on January 6 will come back stronger amid a potential wave of violence that would erupt nationwide if Trump won the 2024 race and Vice President Kamala Harris, in response, decides to "throw out election results"—a move that, according to Maher, Trump supporters wanted former Vice President Mike Pence to do when President Joe Biden won in 2020.

"The ding dongs who sacked the Capitol last year? That was like when Al Qaeda tried to take down the World Trade Center, the first time with a van. It was a joke. But the next time they came back with planes," Maher said.

Maher believed that Trump supporters will become stronger as the former president starts having large rallies again "which [will] become increasingly angry and threatening, as Trump indulges his love for inciting violence."

Chapter 9 <u>Is A Racist And Frightened GOP Willing To Kill Our Democracy?</u>

11 October 2021

The non-cooperative GOP has us all wondering why, as Senate Minority Leader Mitch McConnell has admitted, he is keen to see Biden fail. He has opposed everything Biden has put forward. See his latest <u>here</u>.

If we don't fix our infrastructure beyond the roads, bridges, and hard assets in need of repairs and fail to fix our human infrastructure such as daycare for working mothers and many other needs of our poorest citizens, we fail as a democracy.

If Biden's major programs fail, will the GOP win power in the midterms and set the stage for Trump to run in 2024? Quite possibly.

And as GOP controlled states pass voting rights laws that restrict minority voting, Trump could win a second term.

This scenario confirms my thesis that the real GOP power play objective is based on their racist fear of the demographic trend which by the 2040's will put non-white voters in the majority.

Instead of embracing the talent and contributions education-for-all can create, these anti-Democratic racists are behaving like the Taliban with their women (and the way we did and still somewhat do today).

And the active political involvement of our younger voters, who perhaps see our ills better than most of their elders.

However, the present political situation for the future of our republic is, as many have noted, the most dangerous since the Civil War.

This is a time when we choose between progress for all of us or fading as other nations overtake us.

Wake up, look around you, Folks, and see the new face of America. More than partial equality, more education, and the powerful effect of tragic events like George Floyd's murder only partially reflect the huge positive trend toward more fully utilizing all our Human Resources.

That trend will be continuing, and we can hope will keep our democracy going in a positive direction.

And after the exposure at a dramatic Senate hearing by Frances Haugen, a former employee of Facebook's undue influence on our democracy and our children what will be done legislatively? Probably not enough. Will Haugen's career thrive even as her cache of actual Facebook documents prove her case?

We can see more and more every day what Trump's type of governance has already created. Examples abound but the hatred, violence and divisiveness has jolted thinking voters into the stark realization of where Trump and his band of brigands has taken us: To a unique place in U.S. history where a sitting President tried to execute a coup to deny his successor's assumption of office after his 11/3/20 defeat.

Due to Trump's Supreme Court packing, Roe v. Wade is likely in deep trouble.

Further, our vital voting rights will be impeded, the pandemic will be prolonged by the unvaccinated, and many elected anti-Trump officials have already been verbally attacked and on and on, until if Trump wins a second term, we could very well lose our democracy.

Startling facts: Dr Francis Collins, the distinguished head of the NIH, has received death threats and his longtime colleague Dr Anthony Fauci, now an advisor to Biden on the pandemic, requires full time security guard protection, based on his major role in handling the pandemic!

That is how Hitler got to power.

Your choice, Folks, for now, for once Trump and his ilk get fully ensconced, choice likely won't be yours!

The surfacing of the disruptive power of the January 6th Fascists should awaken all of us in both parties.

Where did the GOP go? A positive quote: Politico article claims most Senators say they don't want Trump to run in 2024.

No wonder, but meantime who still goes to Mar-A-Lago? Many.

Chapter 10 <u>Will The Adolph Clone Of The Republican Party Continue To Hold It Hostage?</u>

9 October 2021

Despite the startling <u>N.Y. Times</u> and <u>Washington Post</u> reporting on how Trump tried to get the Justice Department's assistance to overturn Biden's election win, the <u>Wall Street Journal</u> only managed its story on Friday October 8th on page 4. And no mention in its editorial page or in its usual page one news summary on its left side.

Now we learn that their lawyer told those asked to testify at the House Commission of the January 6th insurrection not to cooperate. Read that <u>here</u>.

Are you getting the obfuscation of justice message yet? Read on.

The enormity of a President trying to pull off a coup stands unique in our history although Trump's use of lies, and illegal pressure reminded many of Hitler's path to power in 1933.

And Trump's power over the GOP remains as its leaders won't call him out as they did with Nixon for lesser crimes, backing Nixon's conviction so he fled to avoid conviction in the Senate.

In short, Trump's future threat to our democracy remains keenly possible.

The midterms may tell us a lot, but meantime it is worth noting the lead Op Ed in the same Friday WSJ paper entitled "The Tyranny of the 21st Century Crowd" which argues that our idealistic young are the dangerous crowd upsetting our democracy rather than the vicious types who stormed the Capitol on January 6th! Talk about corrupting truth. Read this sophisticated deception and decide for yourself.

Trump still controls the GOP and wants to run again for a second term in 2024.

Two years is an eternity in electoral politics, but I would hope that scenario could be altered since I believe some (enough?) of the pro Trump fervor will have vanished if the GOP does not do well in the midterms.

But if the GOP does well in the midterms our democracy's future is in deep jeopardy. Nothing so serious like what now has happened in our democracy except in 1860 with the onset of the Civil War.

Hard to fathom how a twice impeached ex-President, still can be supported by his GOP voters who watched him try to stage a coup after he lost the 11/3/20 election, by claiming election fraud that has often been proven a lie by numerous supervised recounts!

As noted by all the WWII historians, Hitler got away with lying his way to power in 1933. Will Trump keep his nongoverning GOP party faithful regardless of his felonious behavior?

"Peril" the blockbuster Trump killer book just published by Bob Woodward and Bob Costa will likely fail to sway those in his comatose GOP core, but Trump's scary history of volatility and overall incompetence may by 2022 frighten many GOP voters, even those who are less than enthusiastic about Biden.

The GOP that caused Nixon to depart certainly isn't the same GOP today. Have these Trumper leaders no shame? Or patriotism? Or morality? Not evident in their overwhelming greed to take or keep power.

This just released Justice Dept report offers conclusive proof as to why Senate Minority Leader Mitch McConnell blocked authorization of a bi-partisan January 6th Commission, saying it would prove nothing. Nothing but the truth, Senator!

Chapter 11 <u>The Abortion Crisis Has An Obvious Easy Solution. Or A Needlessly Disruptive Mess</u>

8 October 2021

With the temporary hold on the abusive Texas Abortion law as the result of the action to do so by an Austin Texas Federal judge, ideologically unprincipled Supreme Court mistakenly voted 5 to 4 to allow the Texas law to go into effect pending its review of a pending Mississippi case which would kill Roe. Read about the hold here.

A majority of Americans watch horrified at the dissolution of our democracy, as shown by the behavior of the non-governing, obstructive GOP, whose main policy so far has been to block any efforts to solve our urgent problems offered by the Biden Administration.

Do we want to fix our ailing infrastructure, deal with climate change, or find ways to help our neediest? Apparently not. At least most Democrats want to.

The Trump GOP apparently does not want to, as we find for example, the Republican candidate for Governor in Virginia, a rich former partner in The Carlyle Group, campaigning on "election integrity" with his implication, now totality dismissed by facts, the claim by Trump of election fraud. You can read about Youngkin's apparent hypocrisy here.

When will these conservative types give up taking American voters as being stupid or uncaring? I guess they will have reason to continue until enough of their core backers give up being stupid about not getting vaccinated and endangering all of our lives.

But back to the SC consideration of abortion.

As Stephen Breyer said at his confirmation as an Associate Justice in 1994 "That's settled law".

The moral high ground of the Catholic position on abortion choice—which under our Constitution should be a completely secular medical matter not an ideological plaything—to force women to go back to unsafe back-alley providers seems well undermined by the recent reported behavior of RC priests engaging in sexual abuse of children. Read about that here.

Should the SC kill Roe with the Mississippi law, it would be time for the vast numbers of present providers to simply continue to provide and let authorities try to enforce the unenforceable.

Imagine the scenes all around the USA of women and their providers being jailed or sued? It would be chilling to see the undermining of our democracy if one of our three key branches became embroiled in an illegal, inhumane controversy.

Righteous indignation will be too mild a reaction if the SC makes such a flawed decision after 48 years of safe, inexpensive, readily available choice under Roe! It's akin to Trump and Youngkin claiming the election system is broken when it clearly is not, unless the state laws restricting minority voting get passed in Republican dominated states.

In short, is the Court creating a problem when there is no problem, just as instigated by the lying Trump and carried on by his non-governing Republicans?

The solution to the choice issue is clearly simple and inexpensive and practical and legal and constitutionally justified: Solution—only one of the ideologically driven justices votes against adoption of the Mississippi law and leaves Roe in place. Amen?

Chapter 12 Biased Political And Religious Misbehavior Now Blocks Secular Rights, Fosters Key Institutional Destruction

5 October 2021

The recent surfacing of two major Catholic Church hierarchy scandals only proves the adage "Tis human to err". But these are truly massive abuse stories.

Read the latest here and here.

This second story about the French history of Catholic sexual abuse of children, which just broke today is so horrendous this quote from the BBC article gives you the shivers:

> "Some 216,000 children – mostly boys – have been sexually abused by clergy in the French Catholic Church since 1950, a damning new inquiry has found.
>
> The head of the inquiry said there were at least 2,900-3,200 abusers, and accused the Church of showing a "cruel indifference towards the victims.

Pope Francis "felt pain" on hearing about the inquiry's finding, a Vatican statement said.

One of those abused said it was time the Church reassessed its actions.

François Devaux, who is also the founder of the victims' association La Parole Libérée (Freed speech), said there had been a "betrayal of trust, betrayal of morale, betrayal of children".

The inquiry found the number of children abused in France could rise to 330,000, when taking into account abuses committed by lay members of the Church, such as teachers at Catholic schools.

For Mr. Devaux it marked a turning point in France's history: "You have finally given institutional recognition to victims of all the Church's responsibility – something that bishops and the Pope have not yet been prepared to do."

Like the sexual scandal which exposed the Boy Scouts, we know the obvious secular truth that sexual misbehavior will continue—but will it be unabated?

However, the embracing of religious beliefs in deciding secular policies is not what our Country's founders, mostly deists, intended.

37

Now, having anointed themselves with holy water—whatever that is—the RC leadership again excoriated President Biden for his position on abortion choice.

The abortion issue certainly will be adjudicated in this term's session of the U.S. Supreme Court, probably killing Roe v. Wade, after this 1973 decision helped provide women safe, mostly early abortions for 48 years. The Mississippi abortion law now up for consideration by the Court law may be approved by the Court, truly a major setback for safe, efficacy and accessibility. You can read the facts here.

After reading these Catholic hierarchy stories of abuse, one cannot believe the attackers of the right-to-choose to have ANY moral authority to question the right to abortion choice. In fact, these Justices simply should not have that right, but they will.

You recall, of course, Trump's successful ideological packing of the Supreme Court with three religiously ideological justices.

The hypocritical outrageousness of the likely Supreme Court's decision is my principal point in this opinion piece: These dangerous religious and political assaults on the Supreme Court and on our other key institutions endanger the bedrocks of our democracy.

Trump's abetting of deep racial hatred's—remember his "There are good people on both sides" after the Charlottesville assault? And his role in the January 6th insurrection? These are but 2 examples of his evil years in office. But now, out of office, not yet convicted, and in control of one of our two major parties, we stand in awe of how our justice system has to date failed to stop this potential tyrant who wraps himself in American flags and promises freedom when the opposite is true.

Scary, especially now, as the result of Trump's lying, and intimidating behavior is the fact that the GOP's Congressional leadership has stopped governing at a crucial time in our troubled history.

If you feel no outrage at these devastating developments, you must like the Proud Boys or believe the mouthings of Fox News' Tucker Carlson or Fox's deep throat companions.

As too many of our citizens ignore our future and indulge in fantasies, like avoiding wearing masks or vaccines during our current Delta surge, all of us will reap the consequences of these moral lapses.

Those of us who care for secular wellbeing must not allow religious orthodoxy and felonious criminal behavior to stand in the way of justice.

Chapter 13 <u>Bush's Actions Now Strongly Imply That Trumpers Are Not His People!</u>

6 October 2021

On 9/11/21 former President George W. Bush made it clear the Trump GOP was trying to gain power by destroying our democracy.

You can recall his moving speech in which as CNN tells us, "Bush alludes to the U.S. Capitol rioters when condemning violent extremists behind 9/11 attacks." As he speaks at Shanksville on the marking of the 20th anniversary of those unforgettable attacks you may wish to read his entire speech here.

Read especially the paragraph beginning "In the weeks and months that followed" in which without naming the Trump GOP, Bush makes clear the path for a GOP renewal which I would summarize with the sentence "These are not our people."

Bush, no doubt, must now have second thoughts about the bi-partisan surge of anger for a U.S. response to Osama bin Laden's 9/11 attacks by initiating that 20-

year war in Afghanistan, but also how our subsequent behavior failed, as it did in Vietnam and with other "police actions."

I suspect Bush also regrets the continuing bad advice from war hawks such as Dick Chaney, his Vice President and Don Rumsfeld, his Defense Secretary when that 3rd jet hit the Pentagon as the Afghanistan fiasco continued.

In addition, Bush must now wince at recalling his failure to exercise the restraint of his father George H.W. Bush in dealing with Saddam Hussein on Iraq which naively put us in a disastrous two front war.

Doing that 2 front war has been historically poor strategy, as Hitler so dramatically proved in WWII as you can read here.

But to steal partially from Roman Mark Antony's eulogy at Caesar's funeral with my paraphrase with a reverse twist Bush implied strongly about Trump:

These are my words, not Bush's but I bet he wouldn't disagree. "I come not to criticize Bush, but to praise him" for his willingness to say to his party and to everyone in effect "These are not my people" and then to offer to fundraise for Chaney's daughter Liz in her upcoming fight to keep her seat in Congress in 2022.

41

While Liz Chaney is not a Bush ideological clone, nor is Bush, or any other Republicans who are left with any morality or sense of honor for their country, the power center of the fallen GOP now morally destroyed by Trump, but Bush's 9/11/21 speech picks up the main theme of good advice again echoing the opposite of Antony's "But Brutus is an honorable man". Read Antony's eulogy here and enjoy its magical poetical symmetry and power which few orators ever attain.

Again, we hear in his 9/11 speech Bush eloquently crying out in effect, "these are not my people" nor do they represent a cogent way forward for the Grand Old Party.

Sadly, its honor has been conceded before and Lincoln's legacy after the Civil War by ending for short political gain (getting their candidate elected President) in 1876 by ending reconstruction in the South. By withdrawing federal troops and allowing resumption of the Jim Crow era, the GOP initiated an era which lasted at least until 1954 when Thurgood Marshall argued the Brown vs the Board of Education case that overturned the "separate but equal" doctrine that kept all African Americans from education inferior to whites for generations.

As a nation we are far from putting racism behind us, not just for African Americans.

Again, the phase, actually my own interruptive phrase, NOT Bush's "These are not our people" suggests that America still has enough believers in the importance of a balanced two-party system and decent moral behavior.

Aren't we now keenly aware that Trump is leading his GOP down a no-win future demographic rabbit hole that is racist, elitist, and unacceptable? Legal pursuit by the House Commission of the coup he tried to engineer on January 6th should put the former President in jail.

As the House January 6th Commission proceeds, it appears that much information will link Trump with the insurrection as his key aides who were with him that day in the White House have been subpoenaed to testify. If these aides take the 5th Amendment against self-incrimination that surely won't help convict Trump, but it would not help his political stature either. He has been the Teflon politician today, but this could test that limit to a breaking point.

The 9/24/21 Washington Post reports that "Biden probably will release information about Trump's Jan. 6 activities". You can read the full story here.

It says in part, "Trump has said he will cite 'executive privilege' to block information requests from the House select committee investigating the events of that day,

43

banking on a legal theory that has successfully allowed presidents and their aides to avoid or delay congressional scrutiny for decades, including during the Trump administration."

Can Bush's weak GOP wing recover power, even when Trump's political fall takes place? Not if its new faces features people like the Governors of Texas and Florida.

Time for a New GOP Deal! So voters will want to know what its objectives and values are, as the Washington Post's 9/25's front page headline reads "Arizona ballot review commissioned by Republicans reaffirms Biden's victory."

You have made a start with your speech on 9/11 and with Liz Chaney, Mr. Bush, but knowing "These are not your people", what's your GOP wing to do next? Yes, it may be very hard to prove the present crowd are not somehow still your people!

Chapter 14 Do Animals And Plants Understand Birth Planning Better Than Humans? Of Course!

4 October 2021

Sitting in our breakfast room here in suburban Washington, DC, my wife and I watch the birds, mostly sparrows, using the several birth nest boxes to succor and raise their fledglings, who eventually poke out their little heads and fly away to begin their adult lives.

Now that Fall is upon us, these activities cease as we also notice the foxes, which foster kits under a shed in the back of our property, no longer do so.

Of course, nothing is perfect. The deer, mostly female in our yard, are seldom seen after leaves fall, perhaps in hiding, not wishing to get pregnant in Winter? I recall when I was living in Pennsylvania, the not perfect birth control among deer populations, which in some areas were sometimes too numerous to survive Winters, and the Pennsylvania Game Commission made sure that deer were subjected to human culling by hunters, including offering limited doe hunting.

We don't know about our rabbits, squirrels, and chipmunks but we see no evidence that their birth control behaviors are adjusted with environmental conditions.

We know birthing seasons for mammals are regular and dependent on availability of water and food, something humans often ignore, as our mating habits and our means of preventing pregnancies are either unavailable, ignored or thought immoral by their religions.

Again, as Fall approaches the plants in our yard are going to rest for the coming Winter.

Oh, come on, you cry, at my comparison, but facts, something now eschewed by too many of us, speak otherwise, as we daily watch the playing out around the planet in scenes of human distress due to lack of sustainable resources.

Lacking resources, animals and plants rapidly adjust their reproductive behavior.

The consequences of human restraint as to their growth in numbers is not shared by our other planetary residents. We seem to have no concept of limits.

Their numbers are trimmed automatically by natural changes in their environments. We are so stupid to believe the same thing won't happen to us!

And the timetable is loaded for disaster.

The many earlier urgent calls from expert environmental observers, who have been chronicled on this powerful web site, for limitation of our numbers has not stopped human numbers from burgeoning to nearly 8 billion, growing 4 times in my 90-year lifetime with 3 billion more predicted by 2100.

The present numbers are unsustainable. We already see the effects of destroying our (non)renewable natural resources to meet human demands.

This growth will either be curtailed by human consensus or by brutal reactions from climate change or other certain forces beyond our ability to control.

As Albert Einstein opined, "Two things are infinite: the universe and human stupidity and I am not certain about the universe."

Choice about reproductive behavior, observed instinctively by others in our magical, magnificent Earth, cannot be ignored by us humans without cataclysmic consequences certainly within the lifetimes of my grandchildren.

As noted, those consequences are already starkly evident to anyone with eyes, yet unaddressed by world leadership.

Chapter 15 <u>Population Growth's Urgent Dangers Daily Documented And Ignored!</u>

1 October 2021

Daily readers or viewers of our mainstream media news are subject to so many stories that cumulatively document the title and truth of this commentary.

For examples, I will briefly list what could be thousands more, so I will stick to the majors, knowing as we continue to add net new human numbers, life on Earth will not improve.

The climate crisis, the growing breakdown of our unique democratic experiment, the possible nuclear war, the few environmental crises, the worldwide refugee crisis, and the huge human numbers in pre-pandemic or other risks such as adequate food, water, and shelter. Enough already! you scream.

Watching the remarkable Elon Musk's innovations on the Wednesday September 30th WETA film and specifically his Martian rocket intentions—he says he wants to be buried on Mars—we again note the predictions of Sir David Attenborough and many other credible scientists who warn us over and over that the excess annual overconsumption of Earth's resources can't be maintained at current levels even for those in rich nations.

Musk wants to build a city on Mars and then I guess furnishing human supplies would be borne by his rocket fleet?

This comprehensive issue-oriented web site for which I write has frequently featured eloquent articles from recognized authorities on this population size topic. So has there been much other media coverage? No media efforts have yet succeeded to stimulate worldwide action from world leaders to implement the urgent need of placing population size solutions ahead of other key issues, including climate change, whose solution will ultimately depend on the Earth's population.

I am all in favor of the efforts now underway which are urgently addressing climate change, but surely the population size issue rests on the far cheaper cost of offering all women full reproductive choices, which over time would be gently, humanly, effectively able to lower human numbers from present levels to those which our planet could humanely and comfortably sustain indefinitely.

Sadly, most pushes to date for full reproductive choices for women and men encounter many stonewalls. Such examples of intransigence such as thrown up by the Taliban and the Catholic Church and the Governors of Texas and Florida and the growth at any cost by commercial business interests and the military madness of world powers exemplifies their seeking more human bodies to use for their specific benefits!

As human numbers continue to climb as Attenborough predicts to 11 billion by 2100 from about 8 billion now, having grown 4 times in my 90-year lifetime from 2 billion in 1931, the alternative solutions to growth are clear: The Four Horsemen of the Apocalypse. As you know they personify war, famine, pestilence, and death as specifically repeated here.

Albert Einstein said, "I know not with what weapons World War III will be fought, but WW IV will fight with sticks and stones." Some humans may survive.

That's like what happened to the Earth's major mammals and the dinosaurs, after that meteor hit the Yucatán Peninsula 66 million years ago. Countless lesser species survived and then evolved later into among other creatures such as us humans.

So why worry?

All our exact future adverse predictions are likely to be wrong, but like gravity the law of perpetual excess won't be repealed.

Speaking of Apocalypse, like the Apocryphal leaper off the top terrace at the Empire State Building said as he passed the 50th floor, "So far so good!!"

Chapter 16 <u>Abortion Rights Symbolize Our Road To Survival Or Chaos</u>

27 September 2021

One of the many abortion rights pioneers I have had the pleasure to work with over the decades was Judy Widdicombe whose life you can read about <u>here</u>.

You may have seen my earlier piece on other efforts to provide abortion services <u>here</u>.

As I argue there, equality for women provides the best birth control for Earth's creatures to survive. However, the bottom line of success in this urgent need for attention is choice.

In light of the current assaults on choice in Texas and presumably to be subsequently attacked by the Trump packed Supreme Court, I feel writing about choice and putting choice in a larger context might be useful.

Perhaps the current controversy will encourage you to watch in this site the film "<u>Whose Choice?</u>" about early days when abortion was not legal.

The right to a safe abortion for all women worldwide symbolizes the road to planetary survival in a safe, sustainable future or a road to continued disruption and decline into a dangerous, unpredictable future.

Why? Population size, well documented by credible experts, is now in urgent need of reduction as we grapple with climate change and growing disaffections of people who are feeling the pressure of the human impact on their environment everywhere.

You may well be aware of the population size problem, which many, including me, have repeatedly reported on. But to repeat, now Earth must sustain nearly 8 billion humans worldwide, our numbers having grown 4 times in my 90-year lifetime. Now experts such as Sir David Attenborough project our species to reach 11 billion by 2100. You can read my recent book "We humans Overwhelm Our Earth: 11 or 2 billion by 2100" here.

Obviously providing safe, free contraception is vital, but the most acute symbol of female rights to be guaranteed is their right to choose.

The U.S. and the other great world powers seek more and more domination, which will evaporate into a miasma of disaster if human numbers keep growing. There will be no way to contain dissent and conflict except perhaps by lethal dictatorships once or if ours and other democracies have proved unable to survive.

When will that happen? The possibility for that condition has well begun in numerous places in China, North Korea and elsewhere.

And how about another pressure unresolved, immigration? Watching the desperate flight of many to cross our borders symbolizes our plight. We simply cannot, like all other free nations, absorb the growing numbers of disaffected, desperate people now floating in limbo worldwide, as we can vividly see in pictures on our media daily. The need for our democracy and others underlines the long-deferred passage of firm, fair and enforceable immigration laws which, as populations grow and politics get more divisive, become more and more elusive.

Let's get our priorities straight. Climate repair, if it can be done in time, but again that is not clearly possible, won't keep our fragile planet from the destroying surfeit of human numbers.

Can we penetrate the male dominated countries where Taliban type regimes rule or even our country where some religions seem inflexible to persuasion?

Two points. The number of countries rigidly opposed to reproductive choices does not include China or India. You can read their laws here:

https://en.wikipedia.org/wiki/Abortion_in_China

https://en.wikipedia.org/wiki/Abortion_in_India

Second, American practicing Catholics including President Biden are already on board for choice and family planning. Over half U.S. Catholics believe abortion should be legal and over 60 percent of all Americans believe the same. You can read about that here.

My constant larger concern remains. That world leaders keep ignoring the population issue. Reducing human numbers is the mandatory route to future human peace and sustainable life on Earth.

The symbol of choice for women is no longer in the realm of activist heroines like Judy Widdicombe or even now as we are told repeatedly about the projected bad growth outcomes from the majority of well-respected academics.

The dangers of growing human numbers now urgently presents us with the glaring reality of what befalls humans failing to acknowledge and act on enabling women the right to choose worldwide.

Chapter 17 <u>Did Bob Woodard Strike Again?</u>

18 September 2021

This time Woodward (and Bob Costa) didn't have "Deep Throat", just a lot of eyewitnesses with guts to finally tell the truth even as key GOP leaders wouldn't.

Was President Trump going nuclear, as he proclaimed 11/3/20 election fraud and urged his followers to create a January 6th Capitol insurrection?

Chairman of the Joint Chiefs of Staff, General Mark Milley, didn't know for sure, but unlike our faulty intelligence at the time those 9/11 terrorists prepared their assault on the NY Trade Towers, he wasn't going to not act.

Trump may have tried a coup to take another term as President for which he should be tried, but now he wants Milley tried for treason which shows how upside down the GOP has gotten thanks to The Donald.

You recall that we have no January 6th Commission approved as Senate Minority Leader Mitch McConnell blocked empaneling a Commission, something that had been routinely approved after the Nixon Watergate scandal and after the 9/11 attack on the Trade Towers.

Now we can surely understand why McConnell was nervous about finding out the January 6th facts about a President who had already been impeached twice.

Trump's record of dodging what for most pols would be lethal election bullets has been extraordinary, beginning even before his election with his comments about women all the way to his call for an insurrection on January 6th.

You can read about his "Women's call" here.

And you may wish to read his speech calling for a Capitol insurrection on January 6, 2021, here.

So maybe now we will have a full investigation of General Milley, learning about his mind set as he sorted through the unthinkable mind set of a power crazed potential despot.

Meantime, however, President Biden expressed his full confidence in Milley which you can read here.

Democrats turned out in an off-year impeachment election on Tuesday September 14th in huge numbers to retain Governor Newsom in California, which could be a sign that more voters are finally realizing the continuing dangerous offshoots of the Trump legacy.

I have ordered a copy of "Peril", the Woodward-Costa book, to read for myself the case against or for General Milley, but certainly previous exposes of Trump, a driven and vicious power seeker, suggest that nothing is off the table when his perceived personal interests are on the line. Is that madness or just a Neo-Nazi mindset?

The Washington Post reported on the largely partisan response, but Trump's former National Security Advisor John Bolton's noted that Milley's precautionary calls were clearly warranted.

One commentator I heard suggested Woodward would hype the Trump war threat case to sell books.

I await the chance to read Peril, but such a cynical comment seems to diminish Milley's professionalism in using his authority to explore and forestall any dangerous consequences from a person many identified, including House Speaker Nancy Pelosi, as manic about losing on November 3rd.

Meanwhile, the CNN coverage of 9/14 is quite comprehensive; read it here.

Doesn't the January 6th insurrection speak volumes about Trump's possible willingness to pull off a coup, even as his doxy VP decided, after getting solid advice from former Republican VP Dan Quale, that no rules allowed Pence any latitude in acknowledging the Electoral College results.

That alone is another indication of Trump's mental state in the final days of his Presidency. His behavior since leaving office in continuing efforts to undermine our democracy with false election fraud claims should soon awaken even the most venial GOP leaders that this may not be a winning GOP midterm election strategy.

The accumulation of Trump's dangerous, disruptive behavior surely must be penetrating the consciousness of many on the fence GOP voters as the midterms approach. They may like the alleged political power Trump offers, but many will likely realize his presence on a Presidential ballot would be better filled by a Trump clone.

Is my contention correct that Trump's political power is now set for a rapid and permanent decline? Will Woodward and Costa's book have the same impact as the one on Nixon. No, but surely it has caused discomfort, as it should, on those who keep kissing Trump's ring at Mar-a-Lago.

As I have stated before, our democracy has not been so threatened since the Civil War.

Chapter 18 <u>Has Trump's GOP Committed Midterm Suicide Yet?</u>

15 September 2021

The 2022 midterms could be a sign of progress if the evil ineptitude of the Trump years sees his influence and his ilk dismissed by thinking Americans from both parties.

As the nation marked the 20th anniversary of 9/11, three of the 4 U.S. Presidents who presided over that tragedy and whose bi-partisan strategies in dealing with it were so tragically flawed must have some feelings of guilt for how badly our nation have behaved since Eisenhower's 1961 warning to "beware the Industrial Military Industrial Complex". Most grievous was thinking we could kill Osama bin Laden by invading Afghanistan—driven initially by a bipartisan agreement amidst intense post 9/11 hysteria. Then Iraq!!! Then 20 years more.

However, the Trump years sharpened dismay for his major iniquities I list here:

> 1. Trying to dissuade with false information the use of vaccines and masks.

2. Attacking Roe v. Wade with harsh Texas law with a packed Supreme Court waiting to rule on probably lesser but still dangerous restrictions.

3. Implementing voting rights laws in multiple GOP States which lessen minority voting.

4. Claiming 11/3/20 election fraud and promoting an insurrection of domestic terrorists at our Capitol.

5. Dismissing the injuries of the Capitol police and other law officers.

6. Failing to recognize his actions were an assault on our democracy.

The one among the missing at these 9/11 site visits was Donald Trump, who correctly, if ineptly, set the timetable for our withdrawal from Afghanistan, likely as a political trap for his successor since his only acts of governance in office were to benefit his self-image and to help his re-election.

His absence (with Bush, Obama and Biden as they marked 9/11) was symbolically and mathematically apt: His 25 percent core supporters represent the folks who have given up on our democracy and don't want to get vaccinated or wear masks to prove that Trump was telling them the truth when he shouted, "Make America Great Again".

Trump perpetrated perhaps the greatest danger for democracy, as he gave the rich a huge tax cut which exacerbated the already dangerous wealth gap between the rich and poor in our country.

I guess feathering his own nest by filling his DC hotel with government events should be forgotten as minor in light of the above.

The mishandling of the COVID crisis was partly obscured by the heroic drug companies' development of vaccines, which even so appeared too late to help re-elect this flawed President.

Where was The Donald on 9/11/21? He was meeting with first responders in NYC to announce he might run again for President in 2024. You can read about that self-promotion effort here.

While there were many articles about 3 Presidents and other dignitaries visiting the sites of the attacks, I was especially interested to hear George W. Bush speak about the occasion and the history. You can read the Washington Post article here.

In this speech, Bush obviously attacked Trump and his behavior as follows:

"On the 20th anniversary of the terrorist attacks that changed his presidency, former president George W. Bush on Saturday warned there is growing evidence that domestic terrorism could pose as much of a threat to the United States as terrorism originating from abroad, and he urged Americans to confront "violence that gathers within."

Without naming it, Bush seemed to condemn the Jan. 6 insurrection at the U.S. Capitol, when a pro-Trump mob overran the complex in a violent siege that resulted in the deaths of five people. Bush compared those "violent extremists at home" to the terrorists who had hijacked planes on Sept. 11, 2001, and crashed them in New York City, Arlington, and Shanksville, Pa., killing nearly 3,000 people.

There is little cultural overlap between violent extremists abroad and violent extremists at home," Bush said in a speech at the Flight 93 National Memorial in Shanksville. "But in their disdain for pluralism, in their disregard for human life, in their determination to defile national symbols — they are children of the same foul spirit, and it is our continuing duty to confront them."

I for one had hoped that more prominent Republicans might at last take Trump to task. Glad Bush did, as the Post article continues,

> "Bush, a Republican who was president when the 9/11 attacks happened, continually invoked "the nation I know" in his remarks Saturday, an echo of his previous rejection of the rhetoric of former president Donald Trump. Bush spoke of the difficulty of describing "the mix of feelings" everyone experienced on that clear September day 20 years ago.

> There was horror at the scale of destruction and awe at the bravery and kindness that rose to meet it," Bush said. "There was shock at the audacity — audacity of evil — and gratitude for the heroism and decency that opposed it. In the sacrifice of the first responders, in the mutual aid of strangers, in the solidarity of grief and grace, the actions of an enemy revealed the spirit of a people. And we were proud of our wounded nation.

> As President Biden and Vice President Harris also did in remarks for the 20th anniversary of the attacks, Bush called on the nation to once again hold fast to its best qualities and shared strengths, to come together as many Americans

> felt the country had in the days after 9/11. Left unspoken — but alluded to plenty of times Saturday — was that the nation felt as divided as ever, and that Trump was continuing to stoke those divisions."

We can hope more prominent Republicans will echo that last sentiment in coming months. Recall Trump didn't show for Biden's inauguration either.

To repeat my earlier points, no GOP governance only resistance, no attempts to foster national unity, no guilt at disastrous decisions for the racism of our voting laws, the attack on Roe, and the post-election election fraud claims before and after the Capitol insurrection would seem enough to confirm a GOP midterm electoral suicide.

Biden keeps governing while GOP leaders keep sniping—including about his vaccine mandates and mask wearing advice! In fact, Florida Governor DeSantis threatens heavy fines for local governments that impose vaccine mandates. You can read that sad story here.

Will any of Biden's attempts at bi-partisan laws for infrastructure or human needs get enacted? If so, that would be a powerful further reason to vote for Democrats.

For the continuing health of a balanced 2 party democracy, we can only hope ASAP for some new Republican leadership. However, even after the abominable record Trump and his cronies continue to make, we can't yet be at all certain of a GOP electoral suicide for the 2022 midterms.

Chapter 19 <u>How to Solve The Texas Abortion Law? Give All Women Who Want Choice A Ticket to A Provider Out of State</u>

11 September 2021

The two Texas laws enacted by its legislators and signed by its Governor this past week will require legal or legislative remedies which the midterm election might solve, but nothing is certain. Time is crucial particularly for the unserved women in Texas.

These laws represent a willful abrogation of mercy and democracy and clearly stamp that GOP wing in Texas as fledgling neo-Nazis.

We will have to see what other states join them.

Meantime, the new Texas voting law will await resolution, perhaps with the midterm elections, but with the repressive Texas abortion law likely to be long in litigation, I am certain the leading abortion choice non-profits, Planned Parenthood, NARAL and the many private abortion providers who have so safely and inexpensively done their jobs for decades have already started to seek a practical solution until Roe can be righted again.

Look at the U.S. abortion numbers. They have been declining for years, so that there are now less than 900,000 a year, over 80 percent done in the first trimester.

Solution: A first trimester costs no more than $500 and a plane ticket plus other expenses perhaps $1000 to give women a chance for a choice and even a nice holiday in San Francisco or many other places! After all we are for choice!

You can read about the services and fees of a well-established clinic provider here.

We are reminded of the bad old days before Roe with passing of Pat Maginnes this past week. Read her obituary here.

Many religions understand the humanity of offering choice. You can watch our film "Whose Choice?" on this subject on our web site. One narrator on our film is Sarah Weddington who was the youngest woman to argue a case before the Supreme Court when she argued for Roe in 1973.

Let's say Roe were largely prohibited in the US. Much litigation already and more would surely delay complete shutdown.

Assume 900,000 abortions in the U.S. a year, 80 percent plus are first trimester which means there are 720,000 first trimesters that cost $500 and the average plane ticket and other expenses at $1000 then $1500 times 720,000 equals about $1 billion. But then I suspect there will always be a state or states open for service in the U.S. until Roe is reaffirmed again.

Then, there also will always be some open abortion jurisdictions either in Mexico or Canada. If no U.S. state allowed abortions the cost of sending women out of the USA would be cheap compared to the expense of our trillion dollar failed police actions!

After all we spend a billion for literally thousands of other things or waste it on foreign police actions, that sum seems comparatively miniscule in our wealthy country with the private sector boasting many billionaires and foundations worth billions more. A single F22 stealth fighter jet costs more than $150 million and the U.S. Defense budget dwarfs them all.

The number of Texas abortions per year? About 60,000. That number times $1500 equals $90 million. Hardly a blip in cost to show these ideologues how stupid they are to think they could get away with this immoral attack.

Bet liberal foundations would fight for a chance to chime into solving this problem and the recipients of their generosity would love the chance to go on an early abortion holiday in NYC or San Francisco or even see their family in Chicago!

Abortions are always available to those with money. Sadly, the Justice Department lawsuit announced on 9/8/21 will likely fail, and worse, the Supreme Court may pick the upcoming Mississippi suit as a way to approve a horrible alternative to Roe.

Will a Democratic Congress act? Probably, but now the Senate can't get 10 Republican Senators to join the Democrat Senator to avoid a filibuster.

Again, the obvious solution: Offer to pay women the cost of getting an abortion in a state where it is legal.

As I noted before, I bet abortion choice leaders have already put such a proposal together and plenty of money will come pouring in.

When, years ago, I was responsible for trying to find abortion providers before and after Roe, finding money was not the problem. Given 48 years of Roe's success, this funding for women should be easy.

I was a founder, first Chair, and President of Ipas which did an amazingly effective job of helping women in many foreign countries to obtain safe, free early abortions.

With great assistance from a great many people, I also identified, and my employer foundation then funded important abortion providers all over the USA.

Now, with the electronic age, and people wielding their cell phones, coordination of such a simple program should be easy for all providers.

So, let's hope these leaders will emulate the late Pat Maginnis, and not wait, as ladies who are not served in Texas and soon in other neo-Nazi clone states need our help.

The political implications for the GOP of the Texas laws will likely be significant.

Chapter 20 <u>Equality For Women Provides Best Birth Control For Earth's Creatures Survival</u>

8 September 2021

Clearly most wealthy nations have come to realize and utilize the huge untapped wealth in helping and fostering more women joining the work force in every possible capacity.

While Geraldine Ferraro failed to be elected as VP when she ran with Walter Mondale in 1984 as the all-male Presidential/Vice Presidential ticket era with us since its inception in 1789 was then over, but then unaccomplished with success.

The UK's Iron Lady, Prime Minister Margaret Thatcher and Germany's Chancellor Angela Merkel long successful service confirmed the issue long before our first female VP Kamala Harris was installed this Spring.

Getting Donald Trump instead of the competent, knowledgeable, and much more honorable Hillary Clinton in 2016 could well lead to our democracy's continuing anguish.

The current sad GOP failure to even cooperate in governance will be far less likely to continue if our leaders from both parties continue to cultivate and empower women in every realm of our public life from top civic to political roles.

For example, as an earlier piece of mine I suggested, if Kamala Harris is re-elected VP with a Biden second term who knows how long before we might have a female President? You can read my July 3, 2021, Op Ed entitled "Let's Think About Taking Our Trump Re-election Insurance!" here.

The recent ignominious exit of NY Governor Cuomo allowed a powerful governorship to go to a female, Kathy Hochul.

Read the list of female U.S. Governors here.

Picking people with testicles over people with vaginas no longer need be the criteria for selecting a chief executive as the big U.S. corporate world has already demonstrated. Read here.

Still, too small a number of females–less than 8 percent of Fortune 500 companies have women CEOs–but some women head some very large companies such as GM's Mary Barra or Citigroup's Jane Frazer.

NOW back to the main present anomaly: who among the developed world's countries besides the USA select vaginas for special exclusion such as the current attack on Roe by the new Texas law?

Of course, we male impregnators are not yet under attack, but who knows the extent of possible aggressive Texas new laws about males who create unwanted pregnancies?

Can we now anticipate a Texas statute banning males from getting vasectomies?

My friends at the Male Contraceptive Initiative have many options for these unindicted co-pregnancy conspirators. Read about them here.

A good model for providing abortion as well as reasonable sex education to young people is in the Netherlands, whose policies are simple, adaptable, and inexpensive.

This description of the Dutch treatment was sent to me by my sister-in-law, Judith Kahrl, founder of Grandmothers for Reproductive Rights (GRR):

"In the Netherlands, abortion is freely available on demand. Yet the Netherlands boasts the lowest abortion rate in the world and the complication and death rates for abortion are minuscule. How do they do it? First of all, contraception is widely available and free—it's covered by the national health insurance plan. Holland also carries out extensive public education on contraception, family planning, and sexuality. Of course, some people say that teaching kids about sex and contraception will only encourage them to have lots of sex. But Dutch teenagers tend to have less frequent sex starting at an older age, than American teenagers, and the Dutch teenage pregnancy rate is 6 times lower than in the US."

Even older women (certification of Grandmother status is not required) can join Judy in helping here in the backward USA with the choice issue by relating their financial and experiential support for the kind approaches the Dutch have made so successful.

As their web site tells us:

"Become a GRR! Grandmothers for Reproductive Rights (GRR) works through education and advocacy to secure for younger generations access to the reproductive rights, justice, and healthcare for which our generation fought so hard."

Back to female equality as the key criteria for the future of our planet, we now know that human numbers must be reduced if sustainable life is to be maintained on Earth, as you can read in my recently published book on

Amazon, "We Humans Overwhelm Our Earth: 11 or 2 billion by 2100?".

Those millions of desperately poor women are now trapped in limited life roles by males—from Taliban types to feckless male bureaucrats—in nations all over the world. The immigration crises can't be solved without curbing the religious and secular limitations imposed on women everywhere.

FHI360, an NGO on whose board I served for many years, has initiated a promising effort to foster systemic change for adolescent girls overseas which you can read about here.

Briefly here is what FHI 360 is planning:

> "Join a virtual roundtable with leaders from FCDO and USAID on October 6th, 2021, to discuss how both agencies, their delivery partners, and partner governments are fostering systemic change for gender equality in education, with a focus on adolescent girls. The discussion brings together FCDO and USAID leaders in gender equality and education, adolescent girls, national government representatives, and delivery partners. It will demonstrate how sustainable partnerships can maximize global efforts to build back better in

response to the COVID-19 pandemic, support systemic change so that more girls can stay in school, be safe and learn, and open up a deeper dialogue about inclusive education."

A massive effort worldwide by all nations is now urgently needed. It must be aimed at giving all women choice, which should mean a full life of choice including positions of power. To date, most have been male occupied. The prolonged failure of present, mostly male leaders, to do so will render an Earthly chaos sooner than most people imagine, as many pressures caused by the excess numbers of consumers on our finite planet, are creating needless war, disease, and climate changes which will continue rapidly to accumulate.

Chapter 21 Abortion Services Will Be Long Subject To Cynical Political Strategies That Could Further Reduce Abortion Access

5 September 2021

A very wide percent of Americans disagree with the attacks on Roe v. Wade, which would suggest that many are against the new Texas Abortion Law and its likely adoption by states the GOP controls. You can read the attitudes of U.S. citizenry here:

These unwarranted attacks will likely make for really bad political publicity as the midterm elections approach. The law's sponsoring Texas Neanderthals and their ideological bigots in the Senate will certainly not be voting for Nancy Pelosi's Women's Health Protection Act. See the story here.

Can't you just hear the shifty back-room anti-abortion planning going on now?

The only way Roe could have come under fire was the election of the most dangerous President in my lifetime. His long-covered immorality in the media should shock the antiabortion hypocrites, but apparently does not. In my long experience in helping women obtain safe abortions, Catholic women will frequently get an abortion for themselves or for their daughters but still vote to keep others in danger, even helping picket outside abortion clinics.

Of course, a safe abortion is far safer than having a baby or even aborting a later term fetus.

This is of course why most abortions are done in the first trimester, but the 6-week limit imposed by the Texas law means most women don't even know they are pregnant until later.

Having been present at the performance of early safe abortions done by experienced practitioners both here and abroad, I can report that the procedure is performed rapidly, safely, and painlessly, removing a minuscule amount of fetal tissue which cannot be properly deemed a baby as its antiabortion zealots are fond of exclaiming!

Also as noted above, having observed the procedure done here and overseas, I can confirm that trained non-MD nurse practitioners can perform the early abortions perfectly just as well as MDs.

So undoubtedly the political furor will escalate over the Texas law the closer we get to the midterms, particularly as the hangover from Trump's cumulative iniquities gets continuous negative press.

Thus, these midterms could seem to these deniers of prescient and simple humanity to be getting very close.

At that point, these fearsome five Supreme Court Justices, using their high level of legal and political sophistication might want to consider de-escalation of the Texas law by approving the pending Mississippi case which is another dangerous bill you can read about here.

Okay, this cynicism is not unique as this account will tell you about the girlfriend of the highly respected chief of obstetrics at Magee Womens Hospital in Pittsburgh named Tom Allen. You can read his obituary here.

His obituary in part read:

> "Thomas E. Allen, a towering figure, locally and nationally, in the medical field of women's health and reproductive rights, died Saturday at his Oakland home. He was 93.
>
> Even before the Supreme Court's Roe v. Wade decision in 1973 made abortion legal, Dr. Allen was a pioneer in establishing the therapeutic abortion clinic at Magee-Womens Hospital,

where women could safely end pregnancies under the care of a doctor."

I got to know Tom through my friend Dr. Leonard Laufe, another strong abortion advocate, who at that time was head of OB at West Penn Hospital. He and a team of doctors had just returned from having gone to Bangladesh to provide early abortion services to young women who had been raped in that war.

Later he and I went to Iran, bringing along 2 Iranian nurses Laufe had trained to do early abortions, so they could help train MDs at their Iranian hospitals. Of course, the Shah's overthrow doubtless affected that service.

Back in Pittsburgh in the early 70's, a group of us were working on opening a freestanding abortion clinic in downtown Pittsburgh which did open and successfully provided hundreds of women with safe, private first trimester abortions.

Dr. Laufe with Allen was involved in establishing that clinic, as the local PP chapter refused at that time to provide that service. Tom served as its Medical Director for years. You can read Laufe's obituary here.

These 2 brave pioneer MDs really made a difference.

Allen's girlfriend at that time was a young Catholic named Karen whose history is covered in the attached article. Her behavior shows the ambivalence of women who encounter this problem. She after 6 years with Tom knew exactly what Tom did. I was told by a person that knew her that she had commented to a colleague that early abortion was a painless minor procedure.

However, she wanted children and went on to marry a devout Catholic named Rick Santorum, later a U.S. Senator and Presidential candidate, and have seven children.

That history was covered in a January 22, 2012 Post-Gazette story (Roe's passage in January 23, 1973) before the current attack on Roe can be read here.

I will quote part which confirms the points made earlier. Pittsburgh Post-Gazette reporter, Sally Kalson, headlines this piece as "Karen Santorum's past: Let it go".

> "Karen Santorum's former life recently made national news in the form of a story by Nancy Hass of The Daily Beast and Newsweek. While in her 20s, the former Karen Garver lived for six years with Tom Allen, one of the region's pioneering abortion doctors, 40 years her senior.

This has been well-known for decades to many people in Pittsburgh, including reporters. But it never circulated in print here, probably because it was regarded more as gossip than relevant information.

…

Long before Roe vs. Wade made abortion legal, Dr. Allen had helped establish the "therapeutic abortion" clinic at Magee-Womens Hospital, where women could end their pregnancies under the care of a doctor instead of a hack.

"Karen was a lovely girl, very intelligent and sweet," Dr. Allen, now 92, told Newsweek. "Karen had no problems with what I did for a living. We never really discussed it."

Mary and Herbert Greenberg, longtime friends of Dr. Allen, said that Ms. Garver seemed perfectly comfortable with the subject of abortion, even offering to accompany Mrs. Greenberg to an abortion clinic when the latter wanted to end a pregnancy. "She told me it wasn't that bad, that I shouldn't be worried," said Mrs. Greenberg. 'She was very supportive.'"

"Let it go" was perhaps okay then, but not now, as we ponder next steps on how restore choice to the millions of women who are affected.

Doubtless this story would prompt some conservative Catholics to cheer her resurrection from mortal sin (i.e., unmarried in a sexual relationship with an abortion provider). However, the real point of the story is that choice—as to one's religion or whether or not to have children—should be available for every woman not impinged upon by anyone's religious or personal ideology.

We are now in the throes of an unnecessary controversy, courtesy once again from the merciless reactions of ideologues who care nothing for women, but will do anything for political power.

We can fix this mess, but it will take courage and commitment.

Are there any such Republicans in the Senate besides Maine's Susan Collins and Alaskan Senator Lisa Murkowski? Again, the cynicism and dangerous politics that have ensued and will continue needlessly for more years, should be just a humanitarian women's health issue as it has been for nearly 50 years under Roe v. Wade!

Chapter 22 <u>Democratic Justice Is Broken In 2 of Our 3 Main Branches Of Federal Government</u>

2 September 2021

The precious tripod of the three vital legs upon which our democratic government depends is now badly compromised by the invidious attacks by ex-President Trump and his weak, compliant, and irresponsible GOP confederates.

First, even with the post January 6th Trump lies about election fraud and his huge original hyping that caused the attack on the Capitol, control of the GOP has succumbed to Trump and his acolytes. So, the GOP representatives in the House and Senate are not governing but rather are resorting to blocking anything constructive by the Democratic majority. Read here as the Trump lying about voter fraud continues:

Note that House Minority Leader Kevin McCarthy does not want the House Commission on January 6th to have access to any evidence of misconduct. Read about his threat here.

Republican Liz Chaney's appointment as <u>Vice Chair of the House Commission</u> helps but Minority Senate leader Mitch McConnell's failure to back a full bipartisan Commission reeks of an attempted GOP coverup.

From Mar-a-Lago, Trump keeps up his Hitler style drumbeats of lies. <u>Here</u> another example.

Now as the odious result of his packing the Supreme Court with religious zealots, the Court seems clearly focused on killing Roe.

Earlier Justices such as Anthony Kennedy, a Catholic like Joe Biden, came to recognize the enormity of the anti-Roe position.

That Biden has come full circle to understate the inhumanity of being against medical safety and health for so many women can be read about <u>here</u>.

On many occasions, Justice Kennedy was the swing vote (5-4) against ideological impropriety. You can read about that <u>here.</u>

Would that this retired Justice, Anthony Kennedy, might decide to speak out now about his POV on Roe.

After failing to do its duty in stopping the odious Texas abortion from going into effect, these 5 right justices on

Trump's ideologically packed court said "wait, women of America until we tell you what you can do with your body".

After 48 years of freedom under Roe with safe, mostly early abortions in excellent clinics all over the US, the specter of back-alley coat hanger endangerment looms.

Obviously, no law now will stop abortions, only the freedom to have one safely, conveniently, and priced reasonably.

So fixated on their ideology that no reasonable argument can reach them, these were unjust justices, ironically picked for totally political purposes by a person likely to have been asked to pay for this service for someone in his well-publicized romps through many amours.

You can read about their ideological lunacy here.

48 years and now this mean, uncaring minority opinion of American voters is riding herd on the three quarters of American voters who wish to keep Roe. You can read the facts here.

The majority of American's wishes on Roe and many other key priorities are under pressure.

For example, this applies also to the GOP's attempts to restrict voting rights for minorities.

Okay, the growing stink of the Trump era continues. The ball is in your court, Folks. Only your vote against the continuing destruction of our democracy at the midterms can help deflect the ominous tide of neo-fascist and/or religiously dominated governance being offered by 2 of our 3 main branches of government.

Chapter 23 <u>U.S. Women's Abortion Rights Takes A Taliban Like Turn!</u>

2 September 2021

Several years ago, I had pleasure of meeting Supreme Court Associate Justice Stephen Breyer and complimenting him on his reply when asked about his view of abortion as he was being interrogated by that Congressional committee 27 years ago. He said, "That's settled law."

Roe v. Wade was decided in January 1973 and enabled women—even after a decision in a later case (Casey) modified choice —to receive safe abortions up to the time of viability in the 23rd week of pregnancy.

The right of choice for all women to exercise control over their own bodies was dramatically argued by leaders of every religion in a 1990 film you can view on this web site entitled <u>Whose Choice</u>?

The brave young lawyer, Sarah Ragle Weddington, who argued the case 43 years ago before the Supreme Court also opines on the issue on this film.

The decision of the Texas court, which you can read here, poses calamitous restrictions on this "settled law". We can abhor and fear the likely moral failure of the U.S. Supreme Court to immediately rule against the religious fanaticism which allowed this obscene law to activate the dangerous invasion of personal privacy.

The sick and stumbling GOP will hopefully pay a big political price for Trump's "victory" in the midterm elections, as more and more women realize the enormity of their loss of freedom.

Pro Choice advocates have already opined that the Supreme Court will vote to kill Roe, thus bringing to fulfillment the Donald Trump promise.

Here are a couple of opinions you can read:

https://www.washingtonpost.com/opinions/2021/09/01/supreme-court-texas-law-roe-v-wade/

https://www.washingtonpost.com/politics/2021/09/01/antiabortion-movements-2016-victory-is-nearly-complete

The irony of this philandering boor claiming righteously that he is saving fetal lives sickens anyone who has seen the heartbreaking trauma of women unable to exercise a secular society not to be legislated to by religious radicals.

President Biden, a liberal Catholic, has evolved in his opposition to abortion over the years. He is now solidly in the mainstream of opinion in rebuking that extreme Texas law which sets a precedent for many other states to do similar legislation. You can read his reaction here.

Such frightening revulsion has come from most people everywhere for women and girls under the new Taliban regime. The U.S. public strongly favors women's rights to choose abortion. You can read the full story here.

Now the Texas law which went into effect September first abrogates the "settled law" Justice Breyer proclaimed at his confirmation hearing 27 years ago.

It is now up to Congress to immediately enact corrective legislation to return choice to women.

Should Breyer retire as you can read here, appointing another non zealot to the court will become imperative.

These religious extremists, like the Taliban who seek control of the lives of women and girls, must be celebrating this dangerous abrogation of our precious democratic freedom which should predominate in a secular society.

Chapter 24 <u>The Ultimate Nuclear Terrorist Attack?</u>

30 August 2021

A nuclear attack on New York City? It can't happen. But the question of a nuclear war has been feared since Hiroshima.

As we watch the current brutality unfold in Afghanistan with the 8/26 ISIS-K attack, we watch the relentless escalation that even our best intelligence experts could predict but still couldn't stop.

The future seems full of more escalation. As the brutal Taliban could help now in this evacuation, that reminds us that the enemy of our enemy (very temporarily) is our friend.

This fatal attack, most feared and predicted by President Biden, after our heroic airlift of recent, over 100,000 in days, on August 26 in Kabul. Even as the Taliban didn't want violence now.

After our own brutal conquest of the North American continent, breaking every treaty our government made with its original inhabitants, one need not wonder if some Indian tribal chieftain would have used a nuke if he had had one.

Lots of dangerous nations have nukes and the certainty of their non-use is far from assured now.

It only takes one looney. Is there a nuclear Osama bin Laden with money and access lurking out there? Like those hapless and brave American soldiers frisking those crowding to enter the Kabul airport missed the suicide bombers.

The answer is that very possibly even a powerful dictatorship can't cover all nuclear acquisition possibilities.

The literature is full of stories about total human control of the world's population via brutal dictatorships, like Kim's in North Korea are now out there, but unlike the non-nuclear empowered American Indian Chief, resolute Osama types from the angry masses, but still able dissident populations, are appearing everywhere.

These dissidents and all human numbers have expanded in numbers 4 times in my 90-year lifetime from 2 to nearly 8 billion.

Today with many methods of communication and the proliferation of knowledge, some dissident getting a suitcase nuclear device and seeking revenge for his condition seems more possible than ever.

Our own fragile democracy hangs on despite our brutal record with minorities. Witness those in Kabul who want to come here! These folks are like so many others worldwide to come to the USA, so motivated for safety and possibly more freedom.

Solutions?

You can bet our Military Industrial Complex (MIC) has been pondering how best to scare us into another "police action" in the future such as Vietnam and Afghanistan.

But stopping escalation with a proven failed military strategy is no longer reasonable, even though that's the counsel we will continue to hear. The fear mongering from the war hawks, who can cite our vast military supremacy, will claim to protect us, when we now stand humiliated before the entire world.

Are we in a new era of recognizing human survival on Earth that needs new thinking?

China's continuing COVID coverup and the escalating climate crisis and the many turmoils of desperate people breaking out worldwide, strongly suggests it is well past time for a coming together of the most powerful nations for an urgent powwow on next steps.

What better forum for such a potential Earth changing meeting than the UN Security Council?

Can we overcome long standing human behavior and recognize the certainty of our dismal future if we don't act now?

If not a nuke on NYC, the impact of climate on human welfare will be worse and continuing COVIDs are a certainty.

In short, the escalation of more terrorism is assured now.

Two basic ways history could evolve: With a Chinese style dictatorship or a modified U.S. model that recognizes that compromise and cooperation are the only workable answers to keep our own democracy as the only tenable way forward.

Wide recognition is urgently needed about the threats for an even more dangerous Trump style oligarchy in the USA than we have now.

And bigger funding of our MIC instead of our own urgent infrastructure and human education and service needs is insane.

Not that keeping a strong military is unimportant, but world policing will keep encouraging the terrorist groups to recruit and execute their evil acts.

Could better big nation cooperation be possible in curbing this escalation?

Who can know, but as we watch the current symbolic and tragic press of humanity against the gates of the road to freedom at the Kabul airport, must we at least consider a better way to lead human life on Earth in a sustainable direction?

The main agenda item for such an all-embracing UN meeting? Finding the least repressive routes to human betterment for all our 8 billion world humans.

Certainly, the urgent and now seemingly languid pursuit of getting vital vaccinating methods to the entire planet would best symbolize our intentions. And understanding the need for reducing human numbers with family planning.

Is a nuke attack on NYC or elsewhere no longer fantasy in the soup of unknown and uncontrollable human behaviors?

One final admonition on the irrationality of human behavior: Experts tell us that between now and December 1, 100,000 more Delta deaths could occur in the U.S. if the nearly 90 million unvaccinated Americans don't get vaccinated. Only half that number will die if they do. The link follows here.

Does that suggest the urgency of my above message or just the fact that human irrational behavior can't be modified by timely actions now?

Chapter 25 How To Fix Our Image? Get COVID-19 Vaccines to All the World ASAP And Bump Trump?

30 August 2021

Our efforts to vaccinate our own citizens have failed to reach nearly 90 million people who got caught up in Trump's 2020 intense ignorance campaign designed to win him re-election. They are still out there and still apparently confused.

Corporate America certainly is not confused as Delta Airlines and countless other corporate leaders brought down the financial hammer for financial reasons to keep their viability growing as the government's cash infused high in the stock market makes like the Roaring Twenties.

That Roaring Twenties era morphed into depression, Hitler, and a post WWII world of great American prosperity, but also one of deep world discord driven by great power induced tragedies like the Cold War and tragic bad policies like Afghanistan.

"History never repeats itself, but it does often rhyme", is an aphorism often attributed to Mark Twain but disputed.

You can read about that dispute here.

Trump's post Presidency continuing efforts to retain power frequently, to many observers, (such as the authors of "I Alone Can Fix It") echoes Hitler's model strategy of his massive continuing lies, his efforts to undermine citizens' beliefs in their institutions such as government and its mainstream media (Fake News and Make America Great Again) as a route to a new form of dictatorial power.

In watching on WETA on August 28th of a PBS rerun of how Jews were the inspiration for Broadway's wonderful musicals and Hollywood films, I really enjoyed this great program which you can read about here.

Their amazing Broadway and film productions, many by Jews who fled Hitler's Germany, as well as Jewish Americans who felt our own prevailing Jewish racism, still they helped offer all Americans images of what we could be or should be by using American themes until it became possible after Oklahoma, and many others, to do Fiddler On The Roof and other non-American settings.

I noted that Mel Brooks regarded his greatest artistic satisfaction for getting even with Hitler (even if not possible) was his 1967 smash hit movie "The Producers" with its headliner song, "Springtime For Hitler In Germany". We got such imagination and talent from so many Jews including Brooks. His bio here.

Would that some clever person write a similar historical echo in time for the Midterms about the buffoonish Donald, who even as his treasonous record is laid bare for all to see, remains credible to perhaps 30 percent of our electorate.

Now some his acolytes, 2 notably the Governors of Texas and Florida are seeing the Delta price being paid by their citizens. For example, 90 plus percent of the unvaccinated now dying at over 200 daily in Florida.

Killing off your base ain't too bright, but then brightness is not a quality attributed to dim bulbs!

Mel, you are now only 95, how about an April Broadway show or another film like The Producers in time for the Midterms? "Springtime for Frumpy in infirmity?"

Chapter 26 Bravo To Delta Airlines For Its Tougher COVID Mandates! Not A Time for Politics!

27 August 2021

Dr. Sanjay Gupta showed a chart to viewers of CNN on Thursday morning August 26th which dramatically compared the huge rise in COVID cases for the unvaccinated while virtually none for those who are vaccinated.

Exceptions for those vaccinated occur but those vaccinated seldom die. One of my friends, in his early eighties, got COVID and is now hospitalized on a ventilator, but is expected to recover. In our 90's my wife and I though vaccinated nearly 8 months ago, still wear masks if we go anywhere in public.

Thus, when Delta Airlines finally brought down the economic hammer on its stupid unvaccinated employees, I could only say, Bravo! Since May Delta has required new hires to be vaccinated. You can read that story here.

Now on August 26th on page one of the Wall Street Journal it reported that Delta tightened its vaccine requirements.

Quoting the article,

> "Delta Air Lines Inc. DAL +0.10% pivoted to a more-punitive approach toward getting its workforce vaccinated against Covid-19, saying unvaccinated workers will pay a $200 monthly health insurance surcharge and could lose pay protection for missing work due to the disease.
>
> The moves reflect a new front in companies' efforts to keep employees safe and working. Until now, many employers had used incentives, such as cash bonuses, to motivate workers to get vaccinated, or have mandated vaccinations.
>
> Delta's approach instead focuses on the financial burden of Covid-19 and aims to transfer it to those resisting vaccination. Studies show vaccination greatly reduces the risk of severe disease or death from the disease.
>
> The $200 monthly charge for unvaccinated workers enrolled in Delta's healthcare plan "will be necessary to address the financial risk the decision to not vaccinate is creating for our

company," Delta Chief Executive Ed Bastian wrote to employees Wednesday."

This sharper financial approach should be the standard for all institutions.

Many private and public institutions have already done so, but now is the time to say to all these walking plague carriers "Get vaccinated or be utterly isolated morally and physically from participating in public life!"

And to their dangerous abettors such as the no mask advocates like the Governors of Florida and Texas, "Plague promoting is a moral crime which will cost you politically in the midterms!"

The time for bleating about civil rights and individual liberty about the felony of spreading a lethal disease should be over.

To ignore or allow unvaccinated felons to wander among us is like allowing people of unknown mental capacity to carry loaded guns which could discharge on innocent vaccinated people at any time.

Now every Fortune 500 company should do what Delta has done against the Delta variant by bringing a financial cost to the non-vaccinated. Read the actions taken so far by the recent list of those companies from Fortune magazine here.

The nearly 90 million unvaccinated American felons are still out there. They will soon if not now feel the heat for their feckless misbehavior!

Chapter 27 "Ya Got Trouble" And It Got Well Started With Ike's Warning About The MIC!

23 August 2021

Probably few remember, although I mentioned in 2 of my recent Op Ed's, President Eisenhower's warning in 1961 about the growing power and influence of what he called the Military Industrial Complex (MIC). You can hear his words again here.

A year later in 1962 a musical opened on Broadway called The Music Man with Robert Preston about a con man, a traveling salesman named Harold Hill, who arrives in 1912 in Mason City, Iowa and cajoles its innocent citizens into thinking they have evil lurking in their midst. His trouble is called POOL with the town's young boys in the number "Ya Got Trouble" ("And it starts with pool!"). Hill's answer to this non "problem" is getting the kids music instruments for a band which the town buys at great profit to Hill. That he falls in love with Shirley Jones, the beautiful hometown girl and subsequently creates the band is fantasy at its most seductive.

Was this 1962 musical the perfect example of white Americans' willful innocence?

So overblown were the then arguments of our leaders. For example, they kept arguing that we had supreme trouble with the communist menace as exemplified by the USSR's launch of Echo and its acquisition of nuclear weapons.

Enter the "Ya Got Trouble" boys of the MIC which kept huge Federal cash flows moving into our economy to the delight of voters everywhere.

But Ike's prescience got confirmed in subsequent "police actions" none approved by Congress which we can only hope won't encourage more "police actions" such as Vietnam, as we watch another painful pullout in Afghanistan after 20 years of waste and loss of life.

My friend, Thalif Deen, Senior Editor at the UN Bureau of Inter Press Service (IPS) News Agency in NYC generously allowed Church and State to use his powerful piece which asks that key question: Were U.S. War Profiteers the Ultimate Winners in Battle-Scarred Afghanistan?

He opens with this cogent summary:

> "As the 20-year-old occupation of Afghanistan came to an inglorious end last week, there were

heavy losses suffered by many—including the United States, the Afghan military forces and the country's civilian population.

But perhaps there was one undisputed winner in this trillion-dollar extravaganza worthy of a Hollywood block buster: the military-industrial complex which kept feeding American and Afghan fighters in the longest war in U.S. history.

U.S. President Joe Biden, in a statement from the White House last week, was categorically clear: "We spent over a trillion dollars. We trained and equipped an Afghan military force of some 300,000 strong. Incredibly well equipped. A force larger in size than the militaries of many of our NATO allies.

We gave them every tool they could need. We paid their salaries, provided for the maintenance of their air force, something the Taliban doesn't have. We provided close air support. We gave them every chance to determine their own future."

"What we could not provide them was the will to fight for that future," he declared.

Of the staggering $1 trillion, a hefty $83 billion was spent on the military, at the rate of over $4.0 billion annually, mostly on arms purchases originating from the U.S. defense industry, plus maintenance, servicing, and training.

The Afghan debacle also claimed the lives of 2,400 U.S. soldiers and over 3,800 U.S. private security contractors, plus more than 100,000 Afghan civilians.

Norman Solomon, Executive Director, Institute for Public Accuracy and National Director, RootsAction.org told IPS that in drastically varying degrees, the real losers are everybody but war profiteers.

The U.S. military-industrial complex thrives on the organized killing that we call "war," and the 20-year war on Afghanistan, waged courtesy of U.S. taxpayers, was a huge boondoggle for a vast number of military contractors and wealthy investors, he pointed out."

I quote only part of his piece, but you can read all his views about this sad cautionary tale here.

Our 1912 innocents as reflected in the all-white cast of the 1962 actors in Music Man and our then all male national leaders have since been hugely and positively transformed into a far more multi-ethic population to the apparent fear and dismay of the Trump GOP.

If unchecked, the MIC could lead us into more endless police actions while our infrastructure and other priorities remain underfunded.

The GOP's racism hasn't been erased by the George Floyd murder verdict but certainly elucidated, along with major improvements in women's rights.

We could also address stupid unmasking calls against COVID or the coming likely attacks on Roe by a Trump packed Supreme Court.

Of course, it has become imperative for world leaders to cooperate on solving those more urgent issues such as climate threats and unsustainable population growth which hounds human futures on our already ravaged planet Earth.

Yes, "Ya got trouble" but it ain't in River City nor is it being addressed by the "little rabbits" as Peggy Noonan recently dubbed those 35 GOP House members who keep kissing The Donald's ring at Mar-a-Lago in hopes of their re-election in 2022 or the Governors who keep ignoring the surging Delta growth in several GOP controlled states.

Chapter 28 <u>The Blame Biden Boys Have Short Memories</u>

20 August 2021

The hue and cry from the same voices that backed Trump's decision to withdraw from Afghanistan have now reached fever pitch. There are many Americans still there and Biden has promised to get them all out, plus the Afghanis who helped our side, despite the false claims of the Taliban that those who remain will be safe.

No one can know now how much of these evacuation claims will prove true, but the clearest reporting on the situation I have read to date was from a veteran Indian journalist, Rahul Singh, who generously allowed this web site the privilege of publishing his views. I strongly suggest that in the midst of this media barrage and bombast, you read this piece again here if you have not already.

It seems these blame boys have very short memories.

Looking back on 20 years of fallacious thinking about our role as world policeman and nation builders forces me to look back farther than to ex-President Trump's May 2021 decision to leave Afghanistan.

The potential for leaving Biden with disaster to face and solve is carefully and authoritatively presented by the attached NPR programs by Terry Gross which you can read here.

Biden agreed to withdraw, properly in my view, even if the execution of this withdrawal has gone badly due to bad planning and intelligence from his advisors. He now gets hammered both by the Military Industrial Complex (MIC) believers and those who know women will not fare well under Taliban rule.

Just another example of how Industrial Military Complex President Eisenhower warned us about got Congress to ignore its responsibility to approve U.S. involvement in foreign wars. Congress has seldom authorized wars since FDR got approval after the Japanese attack on Pearl Harbor at the onset of WWII.

Failure to harken to Eisenhower's 1961 warning to beware of the MIC has cost us innumerable amounts of treasure and massive losses of lives.

You can listen to Ike's speech here.

In case after case pursuing the fear of the communist menace—yes, Cuba was offered USSR help (remember the Cuban missile crisis?) because we handled Castro so stupidly—while failing to realize USSR's own growing weakness.

Remember JFK's Bay of Pigs disaster?

Then after our failure in Vietnam and Nixon's Cambodian massacres, we applauded Reagan's alleged feat of bringing Russia's Gorbachev to heel when in fact Gorby was already presiding over a failing system which sadly hasn't since thrived under Putin.

Meantime, our "police action" wars added trillions to our national debt and allowed our infrastructure to deteriorate so that now the inadequate new bill—if passed—will only partly solve our deferred maintenance.

After WWII, the repugnant effects of war were well documented and perhaps dimly understood, idealism such as the One World Society and the founding of the United Nations in NYC, popular first steps toward peace and stability.

With all the UN's lack of direct political power and its debatable imperfections, the UN remains a place where world opinions can be heard and if not resolved at least held in abeyance.

As our world population rises to unsustainable levels— from 2 billion to almost 8 billion in my 90-year lifetime and climate threats and decreasing ability of all governments worldwide to govern, we will need more and more UN efforts to inform and advocate the urgency of fixing these already almost beyond solution issues.

I recently published a book entitled "Trump Becoming Macbeth" on the dire effects of Trump's Presidency as he and his supporters continue to attack our fragile democracy.

The jury is still out on whether his traitorous promotion of the January 6th insurrection and his big lie about voter fraud on November 3rd will allow the GOP to take either House or Congress in 2022.

Another of my recent books entitled "We Humans Overwhelm Our Earth: 11 or 2 billion by 2100?" counsels action now to gradually, safely, and non-coercively to reduce our numbers to sustainable levels or face terrific turmoil which will make everyone worldwide suffer.

Who can call meetings on these issues? Certainly, the UN can and has done so.

Many are held and certainly eloquent speeches have well delineated actions to meet these problems.

Fossil fuel consumption partly as a result of its efforts will surely be lessened as solar, wind and battery power serve us in major use, but the embrace of adequate birth control has always brought powerful business, religious and cultural opposition. Will sufficient action to stop the addition of 3 billion more by 2100 as predicted by Sir David Attenborough and other respected scholars?

I have serious doubts about adequate solutions to either of the above.

My cynicism about those issues as exemplified by the current Afghan situation is expressed in an Op Ed I had published on August 17th. I argue that the U.S. has taken its view of Manifest Destiny which allowed its European migrants to take control of continental USA and since have with arrogance and stupidity tried to be the world's policeman and nation builders. How that worked out is an Op Ed I entitled "Poke Hornets' Nests Long Enough And You Get Stung!", which you can read here.

So, this withdrawal is a big bet by Biden that after the media flack subsides, Americans will agree with his decision. You can read what Sahil Kapur of NBC News writes here, agreeing with me.

Will the U.S. finally learn that foreign adventurism is NOT the best path to world peace and stability, despite the power and pressure of the MIC and the companies that reap enormous profits from continuing this failed approach to foreign policy?

Chapter 29 <u>Poke Hornets'</u> <u>Nests Long Enough And You</u> <u>Get Stung!</u>

17 August 2021

How many lives and how much treasure has our neo-Manifest Destiny policy cost us?

At Yale when I was an undergraduate in the early 1950's a history prof named Samuel Flagg Bemis who was called by some "American Flagg Bemis" who wrote many distinguished (two Pulitzers) books on America's conquest of North America, but was clearly a fan of our Manifest Destiny fixation.

You can read his bio <u>here</u>.

And here is a <u>definition of Manifest Destiny</u> which first applied to our conquest of the North American continent.

Earlier in 1815, a famed American navy officer Commodore Stephen Decatur, led a successful attack on some North African pirates.

He returned a hero and when being lauded he used the occasion to state what has helped set a standard for American foreign policy behavior ever since.

Decatur was reported to have said at a dinner in his honor this toast: "Here's to my country. May she always be in the right, but here's to my country right or wrong!"

The exact quote and history you can read here.

In 1978 I was present at a luncheon at the Bohemian Grove encampment when I heard Ronald Reagan close his speech to a gathering of big money donors with that quote. It had great effect on his audience.

He subsequently gained the Republican nomination and was elected President in 1980 with the same man who preceded him as a speaker at that same Bohemian Grove luncheon, George H. W. Bush as his Vice President.

Bush proved smarter than his son, George W. who took the advice of his VP Dick Cheney and other war hawks in pursuing war with Saddam Hussein in Iraq, whose defeat weakened Iraq and allowed it to become now a nation controlled by Iran, an arch enemy, once controlled by our proxy there, the Shah who was brought down in 1980 by the present conservative Moslem dictatorship.

Dictatorships are not attractive, but our efforts to regulate them have proved disasters, except perhaps in Korea where South Korea is doing well relative to North Korea, another dictatorship. As is well known, that war ended with an armistice never a peace treaty.

After Vietnam, some of those South Vietnam citizens, who helped us carry on war there, were in 1975 climbing into a helicopter at our embassy as we withdrew in defeat.

In 1994 I headed a study group that visited Vietnam to learn about a promising method of family planning, which was subsequently attacked by religious opponents despite its safe and widely accepted success, again another example of unwarranted foreign intervention.

Who still thinks, against Eisenhower's proven advice, to be wary of the Military Industrial Complex, that poking hornets' nest around the world is worth the cost?

But many in the military and elsewhere like the cash flow of the MIC. The absurdity of a portion of the lead editorial comments in the August 16th Wall Street Journal. Some powerful people continue to favor killing our way to peace and stability in places we can never control.

The Journal in part said,

"Worse is his attempt to blame his decisions on Mr. Trump: "When I came to office, I inherited a deal cut by my predecessor—which he invited the Taliban to discuss at Camp David on the eve of 9/11 of 2019—that left the Taliban in the strongest position militarily since 2001 and imposed a May 1, 2021 deadline on U.S. forces. Shortly before he left office, he also drew U.S. forces down to a bare minimum of 2,500. Therefore, when I became President, I faced a choice—follow through on the deal, with a brief extension to get our forces and our allies' forces out safely, or ramp up our presence and send more American troops to fight once again in another country's civil conflict."

"Note that Mr. Biden is more critical of his predecessor than he is of the Taliban. The President has spent seven months ostentatiously overturning one Trump policy after another on foreign and domestic policy. Yet he now claims Afghanistan policy is the one he could do nothing about.

This is a pathetic denial of his own agency, and it's also a false choice. It's as if Winston Churchill, with his troops surrounded at Dunkirk, had declared that Neville Chamberlain got him into this mess and the British had already fought too many wars on the Continent."

If that is not pathetic journalism, I don't know what to call it.

You might also read more of my current views on the MIC and our folly in pursuit of foreign adventures in my earlier Op Ed here if you didn't see it before.

Biden made a sensible decision which should be underlined with a recitation of the human and financial costs (thousands of lives lost on both sides and one trillion dollars) of our so called "police actions" prompted by adherence to being the world's arrogant policeman, whose continuance will only lead to more backlash. The human and economic costs of this felonious attack war by the USA is perhaps best symbolized by our use of Agent Orange in Vietnam, a chemical developed by Dow and later used widely in U.S. agriculturally. Read here the ironic disaster it created.

Our political blindness about military adventurism perfectly coincides with white people's too long unrecognized racism, based on thinking that we had all the answers when we just had unsustainable biases.

Biden made clear his decision after the unexpected but rapid collapse of the Kabul government in his speech in late afternoon on August 16th, the highlights of which you can read here.

More GOP MIC, as my earlier Op Ed's predicted, could kill our fragile democracy.

Chapter 30 <u>Human Ingenuity Now Needed for Our Survival</u>

5 August 2021

The scientific and other human accomplishments in my 90-year lifetime are not only amazing but also seem to have apparently made too many of us arrogant and feckless about our future human survival on Earth. Or, if not arrogant or feckless, at least largely or unknowingly ignoring the urgency of the onset of devastating environmental threats.

Those conditions have been exhaustively described in every possible medium. See Cowspiracy and Seaspiracy, two recent documentaries by credible scientists about human attacks on our fragile environment. Jeff Bezos' comment after his near outer space flight was about seeing the need to protect our tiny orb.

I attended the first Earth Day in Chicago in 1970 and had earlier had the pleasure of meeting at lunch with Fairfield Osborn at the NY Zoological Society's NY station on Long Island. What a delightful, caring, and prescient man. Fair, as he was known to his friends, wrote "<u>Our Plundered Planet</u>", a bestselling book in

1948, which marked the initiation of our modern environmental movement.

Still, as our most respected scientific observers tell us, the underlying solution for global problems requires us to reduce our human numbers substantially or we threaten the survival of we Homo sapiens.

The global population is now almost 8 billion humans, with 3 billion more projected before 2100. The population at my first was about 2 billion so it has expanded 4 times in my lifetime!

The process of reducing human numbers so that we don't destroy what sustains us can be done starting now gently, humanely, and quite safely. Or we can continue to proceed as we are now arrogantly, stupidly, selfishly and violently to drive our lives on this finite planet to ends. Authors have long envisioned the fictional end of human life.

https://www.flavorwire.com/315584/the-10-best-end-of-the-world-novel

I discuss this issue in my new book, "We Humans Overwhelm Our Earth: 11 or 2 billion by 2100" now available on Amazon and other book web sites.

This prioritization of population reduction is not meant in any way to dismiss the urgent need for addressing climate issues as suggested by the UN.

In fact, many conservation efforts have been enormously effective, except when they haven't been effective such as the continuing destruction of the Brazilian rain forests and other non-renewable resources. One of my cousins has been working there for the Nature Conservancy for many years, but we are losing the battle.

A recent suggestion that the UN form an Environmental Committee to draw action to this key issue. The link follows:

http://www.ipsnews.net/2021/07/time-create-un-political-body-climate-change/

In short, annual human overuse of Earth's bounties has reached its limits as we now can see from worldwide events reported daily.

I was in attendance at the 1994 International Conference on Population and Development (ICPD) in Cairo as a Press representative for several NGOs with which I was affiliated, including the Population Institute.

At that time, the media reaction was significant, although in retrospect transitory, but of course some

123

commentators used words like "historic" or to quote from the UN website, "Out of Cairo came no less than a revolution", as "Barbara Crossette, a former UN Bureau Chief of The New York Times, told the thirty-seventh session of the Commission on Population and Development as she delivered a keynote address on the theme "Has the Cairo Consensus Lost Momentum: A Journalist's View".

Now at 90, and as one associated since 1965 with many family planning and "population explosion focused" NGOs, I can observe with sadness my continuing disappointment at the vast shortcomings of leadership over these years in making women's rights and access to family planning universal.

We are all well aware of the role of some religions in slowing adoption of family planning, but also there was far less enthusiasm from those who sought woman's rights but balked in those pre-Roe v. Wade battles at gaining women's right to choose abortion.

This was an issue which was a major part of my activities earlier in my life as I worked closely with funding for abortion facilities, for example, with Al Moran, Executive Director of PPNYC and helping Rei Ravenholt start Ipas, which focused internationally on helping women gain safe abortions.

A film entitled "Whose Choice" which I funded on the continuing lag in abortion services can be viewed free at www.churchandstate.org.uk.

Since then, I have made major efforts to add more tools to let women be served, beyond just saying they should have more tools. Talk is easy, service is hard. Politics are ruthless. Rei's premature departure as head of family planning at USAID was certainly related to his vigorous initiatives for abortion.

My boss then was a major Population Council donor in the late 1960's. Her $2 million a year unrestricted grants ($17 million in today's dollars) ceased when the Council declined to do abortion projects, saying its Catholic board member would object.

I specifically recall the voice at the 1994 Cairo conference of Joan Dunlap, who had been an aide to Population Council's John D. Rockefeller III in New York city. She clearly backed women's rights, but her illegal abortion earlier in life apparently affected her reluctance, which she expressed to me at a lunch in the late 1960's, to get involved with my abortion projects then.

Her attitude apparently changed as her 2012 obituary reports. Not unique on people evolving in attitudes, as for example also in the early 1970's the PPFA affiliate in my hometown refused to do abortions at that time, forcing a group of us to start a freestanding clinic which did thousands of early abortions in its first year.

World population at the time of the 1994 ICPD was 5.6 billion, now almost 8 billion, having grown 4 times in my lifetime. And world leaders and the media still don't give the issue proper priority.

Do we act or continue on this downward path unnecessarily? The evidence is now immutable but still not fully addressed because of failed global leadership.

Remember those end-of-the-world fiction writers used to be thought of as far out in fantasy, but not anymore by respected scientists and naturalists such as Sir David Attenborough or E.O Wilson. In short "The Road" by Cormac McCarthy no longer seems so far-fetched.

In reading their articles one can realize the obvious truth of the above POV.

Chapter 31 Immigration And Police Actions Are Bi-Partisan Failures!

14 August 2021

Liz Chaney's father, Dick Chaney, and war hawk Don Rumsfeld 20 years ago recommended this Afghanistan police action which is now rapidly unraveling.

Just another example of how Industrial Military Complex President Eisenhower warned us about got Congress to ignore its responsibility to approve U.S. involvement in foreign wars. Congress hasn't so authorized wars since FDR got approval after the Japanese attack on Pearl Harbor at the onset of WWII.

You can hear Ike's warning here.

Why no Congressional approval? Certainly, partly because it was popular to our voting citizens to have the good jobs that big spending brought with big defense outlays. And hawks like Rumsfeld and some in the military certainly didn't mind testing their equipment.

Similar feckless treatment was accorded immigration as importing cheap labor pleased business just like bringing slaves from Africa to pick cotton was okay until the Civil War.

A version of the Jim Crow racism that followed Reconstruction in 1877 basically still prevails as the GOP tries to restrict minority voting.

Now those fearful of losing a white majority can see that as a certainty. It's coming and we better embrace it, or we could face needless turmoil to our fragile democracy.

You can read the latest numbers here.

The South Vietnam war losers and now those Afghanistan U.S. helpers and their families needed then and now need to be given safe landings in the USA.

To repeat, this shift in a white majority to one which should embrace us all, has led our democracy to a potential fracture point.

To survive the racism of Trump and his supporters who are coating false patriotism as freedom to hide their grasping for more power and the chance to continue policies which can't be sustainable, citizens must work to ensure that these disgraced extremists are not taking either House or Congress at the midterms.

We have already heard, and doubtless we will hear more, from some military figures moaning about our leaving Afghanistan, but Biden got it politically and morally correct.

Can these Industrial Military Complex folks sell us to fear another attack like 9/11? Wonder why after all our military forays into other people's countries, we should be surprised that animosities like 9/11 happened?

I suspect the threat of being attacked here in the U.S. by the Taliban from Afghanistan is very slight. Our continuing to use the weapons from the Industrial Military Complex as we have done so often since Ike's warning proves his prescience and our stupidity.

Ike understood that war is not a final solution unless some crazy nation resorts to using nuclear weapons. We are prepared to defend, but should not be offensive.

Furthermore, the good news is we got a lot of bright hardworking Vietnamese refugees. By taking in those Afghans who helped us over these twenty fruitless years in our ill-fated attempt to bring democracy there, we are getting trained English-speaking refugees, who are certainly deserving of our reciprocation.

The immigration crisis so long ignored, like the growth of the world's population which has exploded four times in my 90-year lifetime to almost 8 billion, has now forced massive arrests at our border with Mexico.

Offering all of our citizens here now the best educational opportunities possible becomes the key to our future, as we realize that continuing racism could destroy the greatest democratic experiment in human history!

No college or junior college students should emerge as some are now with large debt. Compare the present total student debt now with other debts—such as our military budget—and we could easily wipe those onerous student burdens away to the benefit of all.

Yes, there are many Americans who don't believe COVID vaccines are to be taken. For whatever reasons they state, Dr Anthony Fauci, whose credible scientific advice has for decades proved correct, noted on 8/12 on CNN that 93 million Americans have not gotten shots. That is not exercising freedom but rather proving the unvaccinated do not deserve the cherished citizenship they enjoy. These folks are like walking plagues, selfishly endangering others to follow the false advice of those seeking political power from the votes of the stupid.

The future? Always uncertain, but positive only if we exercise fairness over fraudulence, truth over lies.

Chapter 32 Reichstag Moment on January 6th? Yes!

8 August 2021

In reading "I Alone Can Fix It" on page 437, authors Carol Leonnig and Philip Rucker state that on January 2nd, as January 6th approached, they quote the Chairman of the Joint Chiefs Mark A. Milley thusly: "This is a Reichstag moment," Milley told aides. "The gospel of the Führer."

To me the key witness to call in the House Commission on January 6th is Milley who can confirm that Trump's intent was to perform a coup to extend his presidency.

Milley's statement followed days of Trump screaming to the media and everyone he encountered about "The Big Lie" and how he was going to change the November 3rd election results despite overwhelming evidence to the contrary.

Reading the final chapters of this masterful reporting job, "I Alone Can Fix It" proves Pelosi's belief that Trump is crazy.

By the evidence which the Commission will present it will be clear Trump tried to engineer a Hitler like coup.

At the very least the Commission's findings will persuade most Americans how close Trump came to producing a disarray with his mad efforts and should never again achieve political office or power.

I predict a vast abandon-ship based on this clear SOS.

That the law and the brave persons like Joint Chief Mark Milley who made sure it didn't happen, doesn't change the fact that Trump —even if he didn't realize his urging Pence to not perform his limited legal duty of formally acknowledging the verdict of the Electoral College was off the wall impossible—was guilty of a treasonous crime and should if proven guilty (and how could he not be?) deserving of jail time.

In short, whether the chances for a successful coup were in retrospect slim, Trump's felonious intent must be recognized, and he convicted.

And as Milley feared Trump really did seek a "Reichstag moment" which allowed Hitler to take full power in Germany in 1933.

Many others will join Milley in testimony under oath that will frighten and educate all of us.

Chapter 33 Trump's Horrific Record Has Now Been Fully Chronicled. To What Effect?

3 August 2021

Some people read novels, some like non-fiction. I must say that reading the recent magnificent books by seasoned reporters on the Trump years as President read like novels!

Even the most daunting stories of dangerous intrigue concocted by our best fiction writers couldn't capture the narrative of Trump's fiasco years. For one thing those tales of humongous fictional suspense have endings, but Trump's tale is not yet because its climax and resolutions have yet to be determined.

Is he going to be sentenced to jail as he deserves? Can you imagine anyone promoting the overthrow of our democracy not being tried and convicted?

Meantime, we can only hope for the widest readership of books such as these here about Trump's years and particularly about this final year.

"Landslide" by Michael Wolff
"I Alone Can Fix It" by Carol Leonnig and Philip Rucker

"Nightmare Scenario" by Yasmeen Abutaleb and Damian Paletta

"Frankly, We Did Win This Election" by Michael C. Bender

I have purchased and read them all. And have just published a book entitled "Trump Becoming Macbeth", which can be found on Amazon. It is a collection of 41 of my Op Eds written about the period from August 2020, when I counseled voters to choose Biden, the Biden's election and the ignominious time afterwards with Trump's instigation of the January 6th insurrection on the U.S. Capitol and his 2nd impeachment.

I find that each of these 4 books I have cited above offers readers consistently plausible and meticulously confirmed evidence of Trump's treasonous behavior.

Without prioritizing any of the books listed above, I found the 5-page Prologue in "I Alone Can Fix It" particularly helpful. The authors Carol Leonnig and Philip Rucker summarized perfectly the main points contained in these historically important books which document Trump's responsibility for the most dangerous threat to our democracy since the Civil War. I strongly encourage every American who cares about the future of our democracy to read any one of these books. Again, to me they read almost like novels, but with endings yet unknown.

Any one of them will allow you to gain a frightening understanding of how close we have now come to the kind of behavior that allowed, as Leonnig and Rucker opine, the rise of Hitler in 1932 in Germany.

You can read a few excerpts from the Prologue of their book, "I Alone Can Fix It" here.

"The first years of Trump's term revealed a presidency of one, in which the universal value was loyalty—not to the country, but to the President himself. Scandal, bluster, and uninhibited chaos reigned."

"His assault on the rule of law degraded our institutions and left Americans reasonably fearful they could no longer take for granted civil rights and untainted justice."

"This book chronicles Trump's fourth and final year as president. The year 2020 will be remembered in the American epoch as one of anguish and abject failure".

"Senator Mitt Romney, who often stood alone among fellow Republicans in his criticisms of Trump, said the president's attacks on democratic institutions amounted to one of the greatest failings of any president."

In his final year, these authors say, "He displayed his ignorance, his rah temper, his pettiness and his pique, his malice and cruelty, his utter absence of empathy, his narcissism, his transgressive personality, his disloyalty, his sense of victim hood, his addiction to television, his suspicion and silencing of experts, and his deception and lies."

The above traits are amply documented in all these books based on firsthand investigative reporting by seasoned reporters.

"The coronavirus changed the world...These profound changes were accelerated by the recession and heightened by the tensions in the aftermath of Floyd's killing. Trump, however, principally governed for a minority of the country—hard-core political supporters/-and chose neither to try to unite the nation nor reimagine a post-pandemic America."

"Throughout his presidency, Trump cast himself as a long suffering, tormented victim."

"There were a number of good people who tried to prevent the worst at the White House over the years," said a senior Republican lawmaker. "Clowns in one camp and people genuinely trying to prevent the worst in the other camp. There were some heroes here."

"It is the story of how Trump stress-tested the republic, twisting the country's institutions for personal gain and then pushing his followers too far. And it is the story of how voters, both fearful for their own futures and their finally discharged him."

Will these brilliant and persuasive books and the already subsequent revelations since their publication about the behavior of Trump and the top GOP leaders affect the outcome of the midterms in 2022 or the next Presidential election in 2024?

They better or our democracy will be mortally wounded!

The verdict of the Trump years is still very much up for grabs and our future still hangs in the balance pending the results of the midterms and 2024.

If Trump or one of his proxies are elected our republic may likely not survive or at least be painfully damaged for a long time to come.

Chapter 34 <u>The Wall Street Journal Makes Peggy Noonan's Column of July 29th Hard To Find!</u>

2 August 2021

When I opened my July 31-August 1, 2021, weekend edition of the Wall Street Journal, I went to its "Opinion" section to find Peggy Noonan, the only consistent truth teller among its editorial writers, only to find that her column—dated July 29th—was not to be found without me logging in with my password, after bringing up her name.

What she said in her 7/29 Op Ed entitled "<u>The Jan. 6 Committee Carries History's Weight</u>" was a perfectly balanced description of the GOP leadership's attempt to obscure the insurrection as unimportant.

Noonan, in a temperate reasoned expose, chides her party for trying to obscure this insurrection when in fact as history it was not as some GOPers "insisted the rioters were peaceful patriots, that it all just another day with rowdy, happy tourists (who) accepted the protection of the police they now deride on 1/6".

As Noonan asks why such absurd comments from GOP leaders, she writes "Because they were afraid of the people, they now excuse? They were scared little rabbits who finally knew what they'd unleashed."

She closes by saying "Nail this story down. Nail everyone involved. Then, and only then, move on."

> "I hope they get at least one of their colleagues on the record on this: Some representatives who later insisted the rioters were peaceful patriots, that it was all just another day with rowdy, happy tourists, accepted the protection of the police they now deride on 1/6. If the protesters were such gentle souls, the representatives could have confidently refused police protection, refused to hide in undisclosed locations, walked freely into the halls, and told their fellow Trump supporters that while their passion was understandable, they were breaking the law. "March with me to the exits. We will move our questions about the election forward in the courts, but lawfully."

Why didn't they? Because they were afraid of the people, they now excuse? They were scared little rabbits who finally knew what they'd unleashed.

> Nail this story down. Nail everyone involved. Then, and only then, move on."

That "Everyone" certainly must include our disgraced ex-President.

Instead of any apparent commiseration from the GOP leadership, the one fatality among the insurrectionists, Ashli Babbitt, who was shot dead on January 6th by defending police, is now being touted shamelessly as a martyr, as you can read here.

Hard to obscure the truth, after seeing on TV those 4 police officers testifying to the House Committee about their experiences, against the photographic proof of those rioters in action against our democracy.

Noonan's honesty seems a GOP rarity these days as Trump raises millions for his future political actions as you can read here.

With our democracy in such dire peril, we must help Trump goes down politically ASAP.

Chapter 35 Hello, Suckers! Did Some GOPers Finally Wake Up?

30 July 2021

It took the famous night club chanteuse and entertainer Texas Guinan some time to finally find her best place to perform. Turned out to be a series of illegal speakeasies in NYC in the late 1920's and early 30's at the height of the Roaring Twenties, where she greeted her customers by hooting "Hello Suckers" and charging her intoxicated wildly celebrating patrons in her often-raided speakeasies the equivalent of $400 in today's dollars for their $25 bottles of scotch and $32 for $2 glasses of water.

You can read about her here.

Reminded me of those who have allowed ex-President Trump to take over the GOP, except now a lot of them are seeing they've been played for suckers.

Speaking of $400 bottles of scotch, we should not fail to mention the use of Trump Organization assets such as its DC hotel for President Trump's functions.

Holders of high political office, as I recall, generally have put their personal assets in trusts which were managed by independent trustees.

What did members of the party of Lincoln get by backing him?

> Long term labels as racists?
> Being stupid marks as non-vaccinated rubes?
> Being anti democracy like King Donald?
> Being for blocking voting for eligible U.S. citizens?

The list is longer but let me absolve my many wise and moderate friends in Texas who against their will have been saddled with a GOP Governor who is carbon copy of Trump.

My friends there from both parties have long gotten the message. Now many of Trump's supporters may begin to see the futility of vote blocking against a rising demographic tide which will make difficult the GOP's chance of winning future national elections.

Just as the end of prohibition ended Guinan's speakeasies, the overwhelming gaffes and blatant immorality of the Trump GOP have now been fully documented.

Like not getting vaccinated, even most of those 100 million who have not yet gotten their shots, they will soon opt for avoiding death, just as the majority of Americans will see Trump's undermining of our precious democracy as a death they will vote against!

So "Hello Suckers" you've gotten lucky. There's time to listen to the testimony of our brave Capitol police officers as they faced those so called "tourist" insurrectionists.

Some top GOP leaders didn't even bother to listen to them, while others offered excuses such those Proud Boy types were unarmed.

Is it time to try to heed the timeless hopes of Corinthians 13 as opposed to saluting the hate mongers who have so politically divided us as they disgraced and dishonored themselves?

Have I told you before that Trump will soon be coming down?

No, I haven't been invited to Mar-a-Lago.

Chapter 36 Wall Street Journal Page One Article Pushes Global Disaster

28 July 2021

As a longtime WSJ subscriber, I am accustomed to getting solid reporting on financial news, but I often disagree with its editorial views.

Thus, I was somewhat astonished to find on its July 25th page one story bemoaning the failure of our failing to add to our population and others also including China. You can read that article here.

These authors in fretting about not enough growth in human numbers to drive our economy upwards parrot the perennial argument, which now based on dangerous planetary conditions, rings so hollow.

Endless growth on a finite planet is madness and requires a complete rewriting of our present and projected plans for handling global growth and the mandatory reduction of human numbers.

As numbers will, without doubt begin to decline, as planetary circumstances force a decline, nations of the world, led we can hope by the USA, shall have to come to a global consensus on how peace and prosperity can best be obtained and maintained.

How about investing in free education for all our citizens? This would favorably affect the immigration crisis since in the longer term it would offer all of us the chance to move higher in the economic ladder—to repeat–on a long-term basis of course. Let's stop making important public policy decisions like the short-term thinking of day traders in the stock market.

How about a national health care program? My UK editor's spouse just suffered a massive stroke which would have been a financial disaster for this family, but, while a severe personal setback, the UK National Health will allow this patient continuing care in a rehab center.

These pro-growth WSJ authors must not read the news about the worldwide human turmoil appearing daily in their own paper and in all responsible media.

As climate conditions spark wildfires, torrential rain, Arctic ice melting, and water shortages, all of which combine to make living conditions for our historically high human numbers more and more stressful. Then add the COVID-19 Delta variant crisis ignored by too many Americans based on false media advice.

One is daily confronted with stories about global violence as shortages confront more and more people.

It would appear that the views of WSJ's editors parallel that of so many major global leaders in failing to grasp the urgency of these threats to human survival.

I will mail a copy of my new book "We Humans Overwhelm Our Earth: 11 or 2 billion by 2100?" to the Journal's new Editor in Chief Matt Murray, who could see the smoke from his window in his office from the wildfires in Oregon.

Having written so often about this fact of human overshoot, I will repeat my most recent Op Ed which you can read here.

At 90 I have lived to see human numbers grow from 2 billion to nearly 8 billion (that's 4 times!!), while famous environmentalist Sir David Attenborough predicts we may add 3 billion more, but I can only wonder if deteriorating global conditions will stop that heinous addition of more desperate people in want from happening.

Chapter 37 <u>Did Bezos In Seeing Earth From Afar Really Understand Its Fragility?</u>

23 July 2021

My initial assessment of these rich rocket launchers playing with their expensive toys could be wrong if what they saw helped us act on Earth's fragility as Bezos, one of the world's richest men, opined in his post flight interview. He said we must protect that small orb we live on.

Our space flights have given us this stunning Earth view many times, but the universal impact of climate change and other human caused problems gives us urgent insight on the need for prompt action NOW.

Our greatest problem now is not that science has failed to tell us how to fix "Our Plundered Planet" as Fairfield Osborn opined in his famous book in 1948, but the real problem is getting world leaders, particularly our own leaders, to get this Earth fixing process really going.

See Fairfield Osborn's prescient book information here.

I had the great pleasure to have lunch in the late 1960's with Fair, as he was called by his friends, at one of his favorite NGOs, the New York Zoological Society research center on Long Island, shortly before his death in 1969. What a charming and farsighted man. He was, with his book, one of the first instigators of our attention to our environment. You can read his biography here.

You can read more about the scientific case for population reduction in my new book now available on Amazon, "We Humans Overwhelm Our Earth: 11 or 2 billion by 2100?".

Sadly, the pathetic GOP is still acting like Jim Crow racists on voting rights bills designed to reduce minorities votes and is seemingly incapable of larger visions about human needs.

Then we see many of these Republican oligarchs resisting getting the rich to pay their fair share of taxes, attacking obvious bills like a modest infrastructure law which is still pending passage. Ugh!

If America's 500 billionaires could meet, perhaps they could sort out these dangerous roadblocks and work out a fair deal on taxes and the larger issues of planetary welfare.

Before Trump, corporations paid taxes over 30 percent with no ill effect and without increasing the untenable wealth gap which exits today between rich and poor in America.

Then upon his arrival Trump cut these taxes to 21 percent which GOP leaders now resist raising to a reasonable but still inadequate 28 percent as Biden has suggested.

So, Mr. Bezos, as one of the world's richest men, might help gather a world reform meeting with other billionaires such as Warren Buffett and others of like mind, just as Osborn had hoped so many years ago.

I attended the first Earth Day meeting on April 22, 1970, 51 years ago before the need for climate attention was as obvious. Earth Day is still noted but the media attention it gets is minimal, as was the recent celebration of World Population Day. You can read about Earth Day here.

A group such as Bezos could likely gather, men of mighty wealth and influence, could issue a Fair Osborn style report which could lay out these urgently needed reforms and possibly even agree to not give political gifts to GOP candidates who inhibit voting rights, or block reasonable infrastructure spending and urge a fair minimum tax rates for all corporations.

This effort would not diminish the urgency of addressing the population issue mentioned above.

There are obviously other issues which need urgent attention, but for starters these might be possible to elevate in priority.

Speaking of another big issue, astronomers are and for some time have been tracking with modern telescopes asteroids nearing Earth.

As everyone knows the biggest one hit 66 million years ago in the Yucatán and killed off the dinosaurs and much more. There have been many smaller hits since, but vigilance remains our primary defense, as with now saving the human species.

What say you, Rocket Man?

Chapter 38 GOP's Moral Failures Imperil Our Democracy

20 July 2021

This past week several books came out depicting the final months of Trump's disgraced presidency. My recent op ed's have cited three specifically which elevate the behavior of his reign with incisive reporting which tells WHY he may end up incarcerated, but worse the permanent long-term damage he has created to our nation.

At this point in trying to reach the 70 percent of vaccinated Americans we are told daily that 99 percent of COVID deaths are to people likely in Trump's unvaccinated base. This should give one an idea of how much his and FOX and other liars have resonated there. These people are just stupid. After all, anyone who would buy into QAnon can't be all there.

Lest you feel I am solely speaking about the GOP's current behavior, let me go back in history to point out that the evil of 400 years of slavery relates to all of our colonists and their heirs in both parties.

After the Civil War with Lincoln's VP now President Andrew Johnson, a Southerner, was impeached in 1868 by the U.S. House but not convicted by the Senate. You can read this fascinating story here.

When the North's victorious general, U.S. Grant, like Eisenhower after WWII, became a 2 term President, his Administration initiated the period known as Reconstruction in the defeated South. Many African Americans got elected to public offices including the Congress. If racism hadn't intervened, this could have led the nation to resolving our long legacy of racism, but unfortunately Grant, a very honest man, had rascals in his inner circle who were involved in a so-called Whiskey Ring scandal at the end of his tenure.

Then, in a contested Presidential election in 1876, the Northern Republican Hayes was given the office and the Republicans acquiesced to the end of Reconstruction withdrawing troops. Then the Southern whites began their racism with the Jim Crow Era which began in 1877 and extended until 1954!

You can read about it here.

The white Southerners also tried to obscure their defeat by erecting statues everywhere of their military heroes, such as for racist Generals Robert E. Lee and Stonewall

Jackson, which stayed in place until their removal recently in Richmond.

You could argue that the GOP participated in their abdication on Reconstruction as furthering continuance of our sad racial history.

Long before Grant's tomb was constructed in New York City in 1897, the black population was suffering viciously under white supremacy.

Read about the Jim Crow Law era here.

So, there is plenty of blame to go around for both major parties but that was then, and this is now. We have overturned some impediments to racial equity such as "separate but equal", which further created poorer black education, but far too few changes have occurred and now it is the Democrats who have supplanted the GOP in their efforts to end racism. The Supreme Court ruling that followed on May 18, 1896, and that bore the names of Plessy and Ferguson solidified the establishment of the Jim Crow era.

The current GOP efforts in the multiple states they control to lessen minority voting really represents the ultimate fault which must NOT be instituted in the US.

The behavior of the twice impeached Trump and most of his elected GOP colleagues since the November 3rd

Presidential election and the Capitol insurrection on January 6th represents the renewal of the immoral conduct of 1876, but now Trump's creation of a deep and dangerous political crisis has been driven by GOP immortality could potentially topple our fragile democracy.

One commentator I heard recently opined that the recent books about Trump, which I commented about in earlier op eds, would not greatly change GOP immoral behavior about voting and the chance for a Trump resurgence in the 2022 midterms and the 2024 Presidential election should not be underestimated.

Those who haven't read these books, I found particularly informative about the truly gross dishonest and disgusting conduct of Trump and too many in the Trump era, should not fail to do so. They are 1. Landslide by Michael Wolff, 2. Frankly, We Did Win This Election by Michael C. Bender, and 3. I Alone Can Fix It by Carol Leonnig and Phillip Rucker.

And I am sticking to my earlier prediction that Trump is on the downward skids and will for years keep the GOP from winning the White House.

Chapter 39 <u>Racism Redefined Could Echo In '22!</u>

16 July 2021

As the arrest of <u>Jacob Zuma</u> as South African President created riotous looting by its confusingly beleaguered citizens, one need not wonder WHY as the examples set for honest effective government by its first Black President <u>Nelson Mandela</u> and the moral leadership opined by Bishop <u>Desmond Tutu</u> were blatantly ignored.

WHY? Simple: Arrogant, blatant corruption at the top!

Does ex-President Trump deserve jail time? What would that precipitate here? I don't know, but firsthand accounts by credible reporters of his aberrant, corrupt, treasonous behavior should not be ignored.

This Trump behavior echoes now here at home as we watch the GOP's top leaders kiss Trump's ring, fail to agree to empower a Presidential Commission on the January 6th insurrection and fail to stop GOP controlled state legislatures from enacting voting laws designed to inhibit minority voting.

The old aphorism "If it ain't broke, don't fix it" certainly applies here after the biggest turnout, most secure Presidential election in our history.

Meantime, whipping up white voter resentment from his nightly FOX perch is Tucker Carlson, the late Russ Limbaugh's successor.

You can read here how Carlson got there from the page one July 15th Washington Post article by Michael Kranish.

Chapter 40 Cowspiracy Film Confirms Earth's Human Overfeed!!

15 July 2021

One of my long-time trusted colleagues brought this awesomely disturbing film to my attention.

This careful recitation of how cow production contributes to 51 percent of global pollution was information which many of the environmental NGOs were unaware of or didn't want to talk about. Yet as you can read here, we could change from wasteful animal dominated husbandry to much more plant-based diets and basically save ourselves, our domestic and wild animals, and our vegetation.

As of now we have virtually run out of more agriculturally available land to feed present human numbers. Water and climate are of course related issues.

You can watch this lengthy film here.

Another film, Seaspiracy, equally shocking, by these same scientists has broad media reach found here.

Chapter 41 <u>Trump Gets Unfrocked Completely!</u>

14 July 2021

On July 13 on CNN's morning show, author Michael Wolff was reviewed about his new book's expose about our mad ex-President and his chief adviser and lawyer Rudy Giuliani.

Between Trump's continuing big lie about the November 3 election results and his role in the Capitol insurrection, the author appeared convinced that Trump borders on insanity. Wolff tagged Giuliani as a heavy drinker on the verge of dementia.

Entitled "<u>Landslide: the final Days of the Trump Presidency</u>" it gets high reviews on Amazon. Here are two 5-star reviews and one no star review. I have personally bought the book and another one mentioned below.

First, a verified purchaser who gave the book 5 stars said,

> "I'm not going to write about my feelings — personal and political — about Donald Trump, but rather if Michael Wolff's new book,

"Landslide" is worth reading. This is, after all, a BOOK review, and my feelings about Trump really shouldn't matter.

Michael Wolff has written three books about the Trump presidency. As a journalist, he knows both how to write and what to include in his writing. This is very important, because there's so much "out there" that any biography of Trump would/could collapse under its own weight. Michael Wolff's book goes into Donald Trump's last few months in months in office along with the spicy anecdotes we've come to expect from a "tell-all".

Should you buy Michael Wolff's book? Why not? Like all his work, it's superbly written, and is a pleasure to read, no matter what your political beliefs."

Another verified 5-star purchaser wrote, "Like the author's other 2 books, his final book covering the last year of the Trump presidency is full of shocks and surprises (many of them already reported on in the media in advance of publication). The author has a great ear for the details/discussions that led to the collapse of a presidency on its way to re-election and captures them in stunning detail. A must-read book for those interested in current political history."

Another no star verified purchaser was not so enthusiastic writing, "It's Donald J Trump vs. the most vile evil leftist on this planet. Not only was he Winning he was winning huge and taking down the devil along the way. Only way to stop him was the most corrupt theft of all time but don't worry we won't lose not a chance #LANDSLIDE #MAGA." Aside from not knowing how to spell corrupt let alone how to detect corruption, we can only wonder who is "the most vile evil leftist on this planet".

You can read about the second recent Trump expose book here.

Readers may recall my early predictions about Trump's coming political demise, likely before the 2022 midterm elections

You can read those op-eds particularly my first op-ed in my new book entitled "Trump Becoming Macbeth" now available on Amazon.

Anyone who has not bought into Trump's crazy lies will not be surprised. That McConnell and McCarthy were willing to take down our democracy by backing these traitors should at last awaken some of this clearly unbalanced man's 25 percent base and change the beliefs of the 75 percent of GOP voters who believe Biden didn't win the election.

One of Trump's frequent attempts to spread hate and confusion is his effort to blame the officer who was defending Pence and all the Congress and staff at the Capitol on January 6th. You can read about that noxious Trump account here.

Chapter 42 <u>Yes, Climate's A Problem, But Reducing Human Numbers On Earth Soon Is Mandatory</u>

7 July 2021

Eugene Robinson's column in the Washington Post on Tuesday July 6th entitled "Climate Scientists Warned Us" offers excellent examples of where future life for our children will be if we don't reduce carbon emissions, noting "The planet is warming because human activity has raised the concentration of carbon dioxide in the atmosphere by more than 47 percent since the dawn of the Industrial Revolution".

You can read his excellent column here.

Bravo for this and the other climate temperature reducing actions he suggests need urgent attention.

Reducing the greedy urge to continue to use the tradition sources of fossil energy such as coal and oil will be politically difficult to rein in as the attached article describes here.

However, except for his mention of "human activity", Robinson (and many others all too frequently) does not call for the principal and only permanent cure for climate ills mentions, which has to be the reduction of our planet's human numbers.

Others far more qualified than this writer such as Sir David Attenborough and E.O. Wilson have long advocated from their deep knowledge and wide personal travel and firsthand exposure to human travails about how human excesses have already exceeded the planet's capacity to provide sustainable resources for the present population on our finite orb of nearly 8 billion.

Reaching unlivable places such as our moon and Mars with expensive and interesting toys for the rich will not help bring human numbers down.

Until world leaders get serious about addressing the problem, we will likely be only nibbling at long term solutions, as I explain in my new book on Amazon, "We Humans Overwhelm Our Earth: 11 Or 2 billion by 2100?". This new book, following in the footsteps of many credible scientists, strongly scolds world leaders for failing to treat the population issue as the one of primary urgency. The book is a compilation of the best articles out of hundreds that have been recently published on the Church and State website written about human population from late January 2013. Having travelled the world extensively, I have seen the best and worst of human living conditions.

I attended the first Earth Day celebration in Chicago on April 22, 1970, an event instigated by Senator Gaylord Nelson. You can read about his pioneering efforts for our environment here.

Now on July 11th we will celebrate World Population Day. In 1970 the world's population was about 3.7 billion and now almost 8 billion, nearly doubling in about 50 years.

No truer words have been said on the subject as we "celebrate" (34 years of world leaders ducking the topic of population growth) on World Population Day, started in 1987, when human population had just hit 5 billion. World leaders know that adding a billion humans to the planet every twelve years will stress and hugely impact humanity, yet the world continues to tolerate big growth of human members with more possessions, sacrificing nature, and potentially locking in a temperature rise to 5°C by 2100, an increase destined to do in more animal species.

As with our generous distribution of Covid vaccines to other nations, the United States could set a powerful example by offering to give our own people and all the people in the world free contraceptives at an estimated cost at full acceptance about $20 billion would painlessly reduce human numbers from its nearly 8 billion today to 2 billion by 2100, which was the population when I was born in 1931, having quadrupled in my lifetime. Having spent over 40 years working for women's reproductive health as a board member and/or officer of numerous family planning organizations including Planned Parenthood Federation of America, Guttmacher Institute, Family Health International and Ipas, I can only hope for children born today that current leadership will step up and do its duty for their future.

Chapter 43 The Dangerous Equity Gap Between Rich And Poor Widens!

1 July 2021

We are pleased to hear about the laudable intent of billionaires like Bill and Melinda Gates and Warren Buffett who plan to give the bulk of their wealth to charity.

However, as history now tells us Milton Friedman's 1970's position that the sole role of corporations is to make profits only opened the direct path to the unconscionable wealth gap which exits today.

Here is a direct reference to Friedman's view which you can read here.

> "In his 1970 article that appeared on the New York Times, American economist Milton Friedman discussed the social responsibility of business organizations. His argument was straightforward: the social responsibility of a business is to increase its profits. Note that he first presented this argument in his book "Capitalism and Freedom" published in 1962."

There are now 500 billionaires here in America. Trump's unneeded cut in corporate taxes from about 35 percent to 21 percent early in his Presidency allowed companies to buy back their shares, giving their stockholders potential capital gain dividends. And the chance to add more billionaires??

Half the Fortune 500 companies we learn pay no income taxes at all while Biden's call raise their taxes to 28 percent from 21 percent has now been stripped from the as yet unpassed infrastructure bill which is itself too small!

I often met Milton and his wife, Rose, when we were neighbors in San Francisco. I must admit I bought into many of his points of view, some of which I still admire along with his elfin good humor. However, in my limited view of his immense scholarship, he could have moderated his now simplistic philosophy about the purpose of corporations if he had said, "But companies by paying their fair share of corporate taxes could also be a way of being good citizens in a society which after all makes the corporate model work for all of us consumers."

Furthermore, in spite of his innovative ideas with which many agreed, Friedman did not embrace the pioneer work of Louis O. Kelso and his wife Patricia, who has continued their efforts for equity after his death.

As Wikipedia tells us: "Louis Orth Kelso was a political economist, corporate and financial lawyer, author, lecturer and merchant banker who is chiefly remembered today as the inventor and pioneer of the employee stock ownership plan (ESOP), invented to enable working people without savings to buy stock in their employer company and pay for it out of its future dividend yield."

I had the great pleasure of knowing Louis and admiring his prescience in seeing how to achieve more equity for all. He attained Federal government legislative support, so his brand of employee related capitalism thrived. You should read his classic Random House book, The Capitalist Manifesto, written with Mortimer Adler. His Wikipedia biography can be read here.

This of course fits exactly with my (and the Kelso's) views of the urgent need for all of us to have ways to get capitalist equity which can sustain us whether or not we are employed, as so many of our citizens today are not, only living paycheck-to-paycheck.

In 1980 Ronald Reagan's Presidency embraced Friedman's theory and identified the government as the enemy. Our path to plutocracy was then well underway.

Trump's unnecessary corporate tax cut from over 30 percent to 21 percent simply allowed companies to buy back their stock and give their owners an untaxed capital gain, which enabled easy credit for the rich. We now have 599 billionaires and many so poor they are subject to the crazy lies from racist militants, further undermining our democracy.

Then as time passed as so often happened since WWII, all our leaders continued to involve us in foolish and expensive wars like Vietnam to allegedly prop up non-existent or fading communist menaces. In doing so, many of our citizens were employed and thus pleased by the so-called enlarging "industrial military complex" which provided good jobs for many as huge sums of money gushed into our economy and the national debt ballooned.

However, the imbalance between rich and poor and whites when compared to black and other minorities in the U.S. expanded more widely than ever.

By 2016, despite the two-term reign of our first black President, many poor and even middleclass whites had become much more recruitable by Trump who became the treasonous Liar in Chief.

By heeding Trump and his big lie about the November 3rd fraud and aided by the liars on deep internet media, militant racists like the Proud Boys and others coordinated and led with Trump's urging including his treasonous pep talk in front of the Capitol the day of the January 6th insurrection!!

And then the spineless GOP led by leaders such Senate Minority Leader Mitch McConnell and GOP House leader Kevin McCarthy refused to even debate whether a January 6th Commission should seek the facts about Trump's inspired insurrection. Some GOP House members dismissed the historic event as unimportant.

Will this disgraced former President ever be brought to justice? Don't count on it unless enough reputable Republicans (and I believe there are many still serving in office) join with the Democrats to insure his political downfall before the midterm elections in 2022. Killing his political egotism might give him more real pain than any resultant litigation penalties.

Sadly, this right-wing attack on our democracy will continue and could prevail, implementing a continuing state of racist behavior that since George Floyd's murder most Americans are trying to rectify.

If the credibility of our government is eroded by these continuing attacks driven by greed, lying and the reach for power, our fragile democracy is on the road to disaster.

Chapter 44 Not Since 1860!!

25 June 2021

The continuing failure of our Federal Government to govern is due mainly if not entirely to GOP intransigence!

Then in 1860 President, newly elected, Abraham Lincoln and many in both north and south had no intention of going to war, just as many non-Jewish Germans in the late 1920's and early 1930's missed the growth of the racist anti-Semitic cancer that became Nazism!

Most Americans are not paying enough attention to the growing threat of Trump's GOP success in restricting the state driven attempts on restricting the voting of minorities.

The 6/22/21 vote against a compromise voting act failed which placed the functioning of our democracy at great risk if an acceptable alternative bill can't be passed.

Watching the other urgent governance issues such as an infrastructure funding to replace those serious conditions which now exist just adds to this story.

But the utter unwillingness of the GOP to discuss any compromise has led to a breakdown of a working system!

"Can't be!" You say, but what if Trump types are able to take back Congress in 2022 or elect Trump or one, he selects?

America would not then "be back" especially if we continue to ignore climate change, growing violence as the result of racism, failure to believe our voting system is fair and honest, or a variant of COVID 19 surges here or the unsolved immigration crisis worsens, and gun violence continues unabated.

The fragility of democracy was again demonstrated by the demise of Hong Kong's pro-democracy newspaper.

You can read about that Wall Street Journal story here.

Having traveled there many times since the British relinquished its control to mainland China in 1997, this vibrant free market economy has been decimated over time, but now has lost its way completely under mainland China's repression.

Wikipedia gives a few details here, but much has already been tragically stated!

> "The transfer of sovereignty over Hong Kong, commonly known as the handover of Hong

Kong (shortened to the Handover and the Return in mainland China), was the formal passing of responsibility for the territory of Hong Kong from the United Kingdom to the People's Republic of China at midnight on 1 July 1997. This event ended 156 years of British rule in the former colony. Hong Kong was reestablished as a special administrative region of China, and largely continues to maintain its existing economic and governing systems distinct from those of mainland China.

With a population of about 6.5 million people in 1997, Hong Kong constituted 97 per cent of the total population of all British Dependent Territories at the time and was one of the UK's last significant colonial territories. The transfer is often considered to mark the definitive end of the British Empire."

So, America, take down our voting rights and we are on the road to disaster.

Chapter 45 <u>Only More Equality Can Save Our Democracy</u>

22 June 2021

As we celebrated Juneteenth as a new Federal holiday, Senate Minority Leader Mitch McConnell and the other GOP doxies who ignore reality for presumably winning control of Seats in both Houses of Congress, we can get more and more concerned for the survival of our democracy!

We just got on Sunday, June 20th, disturbing new film of the January 6th insurrection which exposed further what the vast majority of us realize is now subject to the outrageous lying by numerous GOP house members about the violence that Trump engendered!

In trying to keep their power the Trump wing of the Republican Party, by passing state voting laws that restrict minority participation in democracy, we realize their true racist motivation and fear!

As the report from the distinguished Brookings Institute projects, whites will be outnumbered by minorities by 2045. Read it here!

And as Obama said here, democracy is in real danger.

Obama noted that GOP-controlled state legislatures have begun passing their own laws that would allow politicians to overturn or otherwise interfere with election results.

"Republican politicians who didn't like the outcome of the presidential election … now want to change the rules for how ballots are counted, and who gets to count them," he said.

He added that "individually each one of these laws making it harder to vote may not seem like a big deal" and that "a lot of people voted in the last election." However, "the violence that occurred in the U.S. capitol on January 6, just a few months ago, should remind us that we can't take our democracy for granted."

He went on to say that "Around the world we've seen once-vibrant democracies go in reverse. It is happening in other places around the world and these impulses have crept into the United States … we are not immune from some of these efforts to weaken our democracy."

Does Senate Minority Leader Mitch McConnell see the numbers of minorities now running for political office? Obviously, he does! And he and his white bigots apparently see their Trump controlled GOP's attempts to delay democracy as their only choice.

By 2045 if our fragile democracy can provide sufficient equality for all our citizens, we will no longer attack gays, or frown on misogyny or allow the blatant police brutality that murdered George Floyd.

But our rich and powerful nation will need to govern wisely by urgently working on such vital issues as climate change, overpopulation, women's reproductive rights, taming nuclear war chances, and, yes, overcoming mass migrations from poor nations to rich nations by helping those poor nations, particularly in our hemisphere with aid based on their meeting reasonable conditions for democracy.

A big menu which can't be deferred by hopes of bipartisanship, which is never coming from the GOP's Trumpers, Senator Manchin!

Jim Crow and its continuing unconstitutional Filibuster must go ASAP!

Chapter 46 Racial Strife Will Keep Threatening American Democracy

19 June 2021

As I wrote on June 15th, the underlying racism felt by many Americans against African Americans will continue to plague us until we understand the remarkable contributions this racially disadvantaged block of citizens has contributed to our wellbeing.

For example, in May, Pittsburgh's first black mayor was ousted after serving for 8 years by another Democrat Ed Gainey whose statement reflects the residual racism I fear goes far beyond Pittsburgh. He said "I like Bill. Bill's done a good job but it's time for a change."

Bill Peduto, the first mayor ousted in nearly 90 years commented that "There was a very strong wind of anti-incumbency and anti-establishment not only in Pittsburgh, it's all across the country". Peduto has higher further political aspirations.

I worked for years in Pittsburgh, having been raised in nearby Greensburg, so I applaud the fact that its citizens were willing to elect its first black mayor, based apparently on his civil service, starting as a staffer at the

City Council in the 1990's and then representing his district for 12 years before becoming Mayor and doing what his successor calls "a good job". Pittsburgh is 65 percent white.

African American playwright August Wilson was born there and wrote memorable plays about Pittsburgh's racism in its largely black Hill District, but he did not find his full voice until moving away! Wikipedia gives us his biographical highlights in a career tragically shortened by liver cancer at 60.

My daughter, now a professor of Theater Arts at USC in LA had the pleasure, when as a production stage manager, of meeting Wilson when he and his veteran cast came to present one of his ten plays, Jitney, which tells how residents of the Hill District used private cars to get downtown instead of regular taxis whose drivers were unwilling often to go to the Hill.

Famed trumpeter Roy Eldridge, the mentor of Dizzy Gillespie, and famed jazz pianist and composer Erroll Garner were born in Pittsburgh along with many other noted black performers.

From Wikipedia I quote part of its bios on these famous musicians.

You can read about the vestiges of current racism in the attached articles. We have a long way to go to atone for our sad racial history.

But the current failure of many top GOP leaders to acknowledge who created the January 6th insurrection and to continue to accept his lies about the November 3 election should abruptly bring us to understand the danger to our democracy of these blatant lies.

Chapter 47 Gun Violence And Black Poverty Are Related To Racism!

4 June 2021

After 400 years of enforced racism, resulting in poverty and unimaginable acts of violence such as Greenwood in Tulsa 100 years, it is not surprising that level of crime in poor black and ethnic neighborhoods is high.

And the attempt to pass laws that restrict minorities from voting will only make crime worse.

The interconnection of these factors is obvious and constantly misrepresented in GOP statements about fraud! Watch the leader of the GOP continue his election fraud claim in days ahead.

And the fraudster in chief and his accomplices show no remorse or plans to reverse their anti-democratic behavior.

Why? Because they are petrified at the obvious trend against their racism which was made more obvious by the George Floyd murder conviction, which miraculously got filmed!

Should the GOP takeover either chamber of our fragile representative government in 2022 there is no telling what these terrified adherents to racism might try to enact to allow this 400-year span of racism to expand!

Gun legislation can't occur until justice is restored. The right to bear arms provision in our founding documents assumed the British might try as they did in the War of 1812 to take back US control. They ain't coming back, Folks.

Gun sales since the pandemic are up so that the number of guns now owned exceeds our 340 million population.

Bottom line: Only when white fear is quelled with appropriate white behavior will sensible gun legislation be possible.

About The Author

Former U.S. Navy officer, banker and venture capitalist, Donald A. Collins, a freelance writer living in Washington, DC., has spent over 40 years working for women's reproductive health as a board member and/or officer of numerous family planning organizations including Planned Parenthood Federation of America, Guttmacher Institute, Family Health International and Ipas. Yale undergraduate, NYU MBA.

About the Book

This book is a compilation of the best recent articles (written from June 2021) out of his hundreds published on the Church and State website. Collins has a unique perspective of close to four generations of experiencing human progress on planet earth. A student of history, he has travelled the world extensively and watched humanity thrive and backslide in many countries over decades. He surmises that the failure of humanity would be accelerated by the loss of the American democratic experiment to a dictator who seized power away from the people. With America safe, he recommends, that the best way to combat climate change is for the United States to set an example by giving its people and all the people on planet earth free contraceptives to empower them to voluntarily control their fertility for their own benefit. He estimates that reducing human population by 80 million per year (instead of adding 80 million per year as we do now) would reduce our human population benignly (by simply not birthing unplanned children) so that we would go from nearly 8 billion today to 2 billion by 2100.

Other Books by the Author

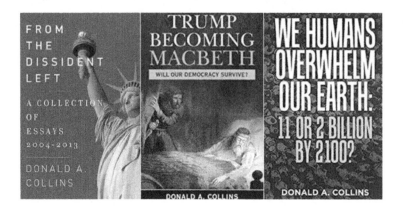